BUILDING SECURITY IN EUROPE

Military Confidence-Building in Europe

Rolf Berg

Developing a Confidence-Building System in East-West Relations: Europe and the CSCE

Adam-Daniel Rotfeld

Rolf Berg, a Resident Fellow at the Institute for East-West Security Studies in 1984/85, is Deputy Chief of Mission at the Royal Norwegian Embassy in Vienna.

Adam-Daniel Rotfeld, a Resident Fellow at the Institute for East-West Security Studies in 1984/85, is Head of the European Security Department of the Polish Institute of International Affairs, Warsaw.

Contents

Foreword

Confidence-building measures (CBMs) are neither new nor dramatic; indeed, a number of arms control specialists consider them, at best, of only marginal utility. Certainly, CBMs will not lead to an immediate reduction in the quantity of weapons. However, if the cause of insecurity in Europe is rooted not only in the quantity of weapons on the continent but in a deep-seated mistrust and suspicion between two opposing political systems and military alliances, then CBMs do have a role to play — and an important role. The major stumbling block to confidence-building measures has been one of interpretation: the East places much greater emphasis on the political and philosophical considerations, while the West emphasizes the military significance of verifiable measures.

This monograph is the result of the work of two Resident Fellows at the Institute for East-West Security Studies, one a Pole and the other a Norwegian. Both worked in New York as part of a group of Resident Fellows in the 1984/85 academic year. Although written independently, the papers were deemed to be compatible, and their approach to building confidence and security in Europe is compelling. Their treatment of the historical background of building security in Europe, including the Stockholm conference, is supplemented with a valuable appendix containing hard-to-find documents and proposals.

The papers seem to begin from opposite ends of the spectrum, but each author concludes that a purely military approach to CBMs is inadequate. They agree that confidence-building measures should not be seen as a panacea for the insecurity that permeates East-West relations, but rather as an instrument for institutionalizing confidence and reducing suspicions in the political, economic and humanitarian, as well as military fields.

Adam-Daniel Rotfeld is Head of the European Security Department in the Polish Institute of International Affairs and a member of the Executive Committee of the Polish Public Committee for European Security and Cooperation. He served as a member of the Polish delegation to the CSCE in Belgrade and Madrid, and has published widely in the East and West on European security matters.

Rolf Berg, a career diplomat in the Royal Ministry of Foreign Affairs in Oslo, was Director of the Security Policy, Arms Control and Disarmament Division in the Department of Planning and Research at the Ministry. He also was Secretary of the Norwegian Advisory Committee on Arms Control and Disarmament and served in various Norwegian delegations to arms control conferences, including the CDE in Stockholm.

The authors wish to give particular appreciation to Dr. Allen Lynch, Research Associate at the Institute, for his meticulous editing of the papers in both draft and final versions. Appreciation is also paid to the Institute's Director of Studies, Dr. F. Stephen Larrabee, and his colleagues for their advice and criticism of the manuscripts. The papers benefited greatly from the diverse perspectives brought to the review process by the Institute's 1984/85 Resident Fellows.

The Institute gratefully acknowledges the Ford Foundation and the Alfried Krupp von Bohlen und Halbach-Foundation for providing funds for this study, including stipends for Dr. Rotfeld and Mr. Berg during their residency in New York, and for the publication and distribution of this monograph.

The views in the monograph are solely those of the authors and should not be ascribed to the Ford or Alfried Krupp von Bohlen und Halbach Foundations, or to the directors, officers, and other staff members of the Institute for East-West Security Studies.

John Edwin Mroz
President

July 1986
New York

Introduction

In the last two decades arms control has been at the center of East-West relations. Most of the effort in arms control, however, has focused on constraining or reducing the number and types of weapons. Relatively little attention has been paid to the question of constraining military operations or preventing conflicts that could arise out of miscalculation and misperception. However, as several recent studies have suggested, today the most likely path to a war between the superpowers, especially a nuclear war, is a crisis that escalates out of control because of miscalculation, poor communication or accident.[1] Moreover, the number of weapons — the typical focus of arms control negotiations — is only one indicator of military power. Of equal, if not greater importance, is the configuration of forces and the ways in which they can be used, particularly the capacity for surprise attack.

This recognition has led to growing interest among policy-makers and specialists in "confidence-building measures", or CBMs. Unlike arms control measures, CBMs do not aim at the actual reduction of armaments or manpower. Rather, they are designed to regulate the *operations* of military forces and to provide reassurance about military *intentions*. In particular, they seek to reduce the possibility of an accidental confrontation through miscalculation or failure of communication, as well as to diminish the danger of surprise attack. In some cases, confidence-building measures may also seek to constrain military activity and military options.

The two studies in this volume — the first by Rolf Berg of Norway, the second by Adam-Daniel Rotfeld of Poland — examine the role that confidence-building measures can play in enhancing East-West security. Both papers were written while the authors were Resident Fellows at the Institute for East-West Security Studies in 1984/85 and are part of a larger effort that the Institute has undertaken on confidence-building

---

[1]William Langer Ury and Richard Smoke, *Beyond the Hotline: Controlling a Nuclear Crisis* (Cambridge, MA: Harvard Law School, 1984), pp. 12-13. See also Graham Allison, Albert Carnesale and Joseph Nye, *Hawks, Doves and Owls* (New York: Norton, 1985).

measures in the past few years.[2] Both authors also bring considerable experience to bear on the problem, having worked for their respective CSCE delegations on these issues for a number of years. While their perspectives are different — Berg emphasizes the need for specific military-technical measures while Rotfeld takes a broader political approach — both agree on the need for a balanced approach to the role that confidence-building measures can play in enhancing European security. Moreover, both clearly recognize that CBMs are no panacea. They cannot overcome deeply rooted ideological differences between the two blocs or transform the basic nature of the superpower relationship, which is likely to remain competitive for the foreseeable future. Nor are they a substitute for arms control. However, in small but important ways CBMs can contribute to stabilizing East-West relations by reducing the proximate causes of war and creating greater assurance about the intentions of the other side.

This volume appears at a particularly propitious moment. The Conference on Confidence- and Security-Building Measures and Disarmament in Europe (CDE) in Stockholm is moving into its final phase. A CSCE follow-up meeting is scheduled to be held in Vienna in November 1986 to discuss, among other things, the results of the Stockholm talks and the possible content of a second stage of the CDE. At the same time, conventional arms control has been given new impetus by several major new Soviet initiatives, particularly the proposals put forward by the Political Consultative Committee of the Warsaw Treaty Organization at its meeting in Budapest in mid-June 1986. These proposals contain a number of new elements, particularly the call for a widening of the negotiating zone and the inclusion of tactical nuclear aircraft in the MBFR conventional arms talks. While the full import of these proposals is not yet clear, at a minimum they suggest that the Soviet Union has begun to rethink some of its past approaches to conventional arms control. In short, both CDE and MBFR seem to be entering a new phase. The issues raised

---

[2]See F. Stephen Larrabee and Dietrich Stobbe (eds.), *Confidence-Building Measures in Europe.* East-West Monograph Number One (New York: Institute for East-West Security Studies, 1983); F. Stephen Larrabee and Allen Lynch, *Confidence-Building Measures and U.S.-Soviet Relations,* Occasional Paper Number One (New York: Institute for East-West Security Studies, 1986); and Allen Lynch, *Confidence-Building in the 1980s: A Conference Report* (New York: Institute for East-West Security Studies and York University Research Programme in Strategic Studies, November 1985).

by Berg and Rotfeld, however, are hardly likely to disappear. On the contrary, they may become even more relevant in this new phase.

As both authors point out, many of the types of CBMs now being negotiated in Stockholm are not new; they have been on the diplomatic agenda for nearly 30 years. At the root of the difficulty in hammering out an accord is the fact that the two sides have different and largely competing philosophies. The West has traditionally taken a military-technical approach to the problem of confidence-building, emphazing measures of notification, observation and verification, which it argues would make military activities more predictable, and thus less threatening. The East, on the other hand, has taken a basically political approach, arguing that measures aimed at openness and transparency can only be useful once a broader political understanding has been achieved. They have feared that openness could be used for intelligence gathering, which could facilitate rather than reduce the prospects for surprise attack. There is thus a built-in friction in the negotiating process, which has inhibited, and continues to inhibit, progress toward a mutually satisfactory agreement.

Given these fundamental differences in approach to confidence-building, any agreement emerging from the Stockholm talks will have to be a compromise and include a combination of specific military-technical measures and some political-declaratory measures, particularly related to the non-use of force. Over the last two years there has, in fact, been some movement in this direction. In his speech in Dublin in June 1984, President Reagan indicated U.S. willingness to discuss incorporation of a non-use of force declaration into a Final Document that contains verifiable and militarily significant CBMs, which would give such a pledge real teeth. For its part the Soviet Union has recently shown a willingness to compromise, dropping the demands contained in its original package presented in Stockholm, such as the inclusion of a pledge on no-first-use of nuclear weapons, the elimination of chemical weapons, and the establishment of nuclear weapons-free zones in various parts of Europe. In January 1986, Soviet General Secretary Gorbachev also proposed postponing notification of naval activities to the next stage of the CDE. Hence the basis for a compromise exists. The question is really one of political will more than anything else.

Yet even if an agreement can finally be reached, the results are likely to be rather limited and modest: some agreement on notification of maneuvers (the question is really at what level); an improvement in the working conditions for military observers; some improvement in the exchange of militarily relevant information, particularly the exchange of annual forecasts of military activities; and probably a pledge of non-use of force tied to some of the measures mentioned above. Given the fundamental differences in approach, and the little time remaining until the Vienna Review Conference (November 1986), anything more substantial will have to await the second stage of the CDE — if there is one.

Many in the West, especially in the U.S., may see the modest results likely to emerge from Stockholm as cause for disappointment, even for abandoning the CSCE process entirely. And certainly if one looks at the results to date there are some grounds for disappointment. But before rushing to conclude that the whole exercise has been fruitless, it would be well to recognize the benefits that have accrued from the process. The measures likely to be agreed upon provide in small but important ways a means for enhancing European security and reducing the prospect of surprise attack. They also provide important building blocks for the future; the challenge will be to progress to a confidence- and security-building regime that places real *constraints* on military activities, and thus on the role of armed force in international relations. Moreover, the CDE process has given the smaller countries of Europe, especially the neutral and non-aligned (N/NA), a voice in shaping the European security order that they would not otherwise have had. Indeed, as Rotfeld points out, the N/NA countries have played a key role in keeping the CDE process alive and moving forward.

Discussion of a second stage of the CDE inevitably raises the question of the relationship of such an exercise to the MBFR negotiations in Vienna on the reduction of conventional forces, particularly the prospects for a possible merger of the two negotiations. This issue has been given all the more currency by the recent Soviet initiatives, particularly those launched by Soviet General Secretary Mikhail Gorbachev in his speech in East Berlin on April 18, 1986, and more recently by the proposals contained in the communique issued by the Political Consultative Committee of the Warsaw Treaty Organization at its meeting in Budapest in mid-June. The "Budapest Appeal" contained a number of new elements, including: (1) a suggestion for broadening the zone of negotiations to include the European part of the Soviet Union; (2) a call for significant manpower reductions — 500,000 men by 1990; (3) the inclusion of tactical aircraft in the negotiations; and (4) an invitation to include neutral and non-aligned countries in the negotiations. Indeed, the Soviet proposal — especially the suggestion that the forum be broadened to include the neutral and non-aligned — suggests that the Soviets may favor a merger of CDE and MBFR at some point. This would be in keeping with past Soviet policy, which since the 1950s has often proposed "pan-European" approaches to European security problems.

Such an approach might find an echo in some quarters in the West. Many neutral and non-aligned countries would probably favor it, since it would give them a more enhanced role in East-West security matters. Some Western countries might also see advantages in it. The French, for instance, have always felt the zone of application in MBFR was too narrow, while the West Germans have traditionally had an aversion to "special zones", in which they would appear to be singled out.

In principle, the idea of merging the two negotiations may have some merit, especially in light of the long-standing deadlock in MBFR. As Berg suggests, there are a variety of ways this might be done. One would be to transfer MBFR Associated Measures 1 and 2 (notification of out-of-garrison activities and exchange of military observers) from Vienna to Stockholm. These measures have a wider range of applicability than the MBFR zone area and might be more easily negotiable inside a second-stage CDE. Another possibility suggested by Berg would be to conclude a modest agreement in both CDE and MBFR and then merge the two negotiations. (The recent Warsaw Treaty Organization proposals announced in Budapest in June, which emphasize large-scale reductions and the inclusion of tactical aircraft, would seem to go in the opposite direction, however, and make the rapid conclusion of any modest MBFR agreement virtually impossible.) A third option would be to change the negotiating format of both negotiations altogether, converting the MBFR negotiations into a forum for East-West military discussion on strategies and doctrine, while transferring the troop reduction functions to a second stage of the CDE.

All these proposals deserve careful consideration. At the same time one should avoid the illusion that the basic problems facing the negotiators in Vienna can be resolved by simply changing the negotiating format. Indeed, the inclusion of nearly two dozen additional states might severely complicate the negotiations, making consensus impossible. If the 35 nations currently participating in the CDE in Stockholm have such a hard time agreeing on a few very modest measures related to notification of maneuvers and exchange of militarily relevant information, how are they going to agree on much more sensitive issues, such as large reductions of men and equipment and the inclusion in the negotiations of nuclear weapons? Thus, rather than enhancing the prospects for arms control, the idea of merging MBFR and CDE could prove a prescription for sustained stalemate.

In the final analysis, however, progress in Stockholm, Vienna or any new forum will depend to a large extent on developments elsewhere, especially the state of U.S.-Soviet relations. An improvement in U.S.-Soviet relations, especially progress in the arms negotiations in Geneva on limiting strategic weapons, could give the talks in Stockholm and Vienna greater impetus. As both contributions in this volume make clear, the negotiations in Stockholm and Vienna cannot be conducted in a vacuum. They are part of a larger political process. To be successful they must be integrated into a broader strategy for managing and stabilizing East-West relations. Otherwise, the ability of confidence-building measures to make a meaningful contribution to enhancing East-West security will remain slight.

F. Stephen Larrabee
Vice President and Director of Studies

New York
July 1986

MILITARY CONFIDENCE-BUILDING IN EUROPE

Rolf Berg

The views expressed in this chapter are the personal views of the author, and do not necessarily reflect the views of the Norwegian Ministry of Foreign Affairs or of the Norwegian Government.

Contents

I.

Introduction

The idea of building confidence in order to enhance security is not new. A number of arms control agreements in force contain formal confidence-building measures (CBMs) that furnish codes of conduct for specific military situations (such as maneuvers), call for the exchange of information designed to provide reassurance about peaceful intentions, and suggest guidelines for the regulation of states' behavior in crises. These include the military provisions of the Helsinki Final Act (1975), the various U.S.-Soviet "Hotline" agreements, and the 1972 U.S.-Soviet accord covering incidents at sea.

Though the concept of confidence-building in Europe is tied mainly to the Conference on Security and Cooperation in Europe (CSCE), the diplomatic history of negotiating CBMs in Europe is fairly long. Various naval agreements in the 1930s contained such "CBMs" as provisions for the exchange of information on naval construction and expenditures. Virtually the same groups of proposals now under discussion at the Stockholm Conference, such as exchange of information, notification of military activities, observation/verification and such declaratory measures as the proposal for a treaty on the non-use of force, have been on the European security agenda at least since the 1950s, and have been consistently advocated as measures that would stabilize the military situation and pave the way for disarmament. The link between confidence, security and disarmament has always been there.

Although solidly entrenched in the League of Nations Convenant, the Locarno Treaty (1924) and the Paris Peace Pact (1928), proposals for the non-use of force and non-aggression treaties were actively discussed within the framework of the League of Nations in the 1930s, which, it was argued, "should in no way weaken, but on the contrary, should expressly reaffirm existing obligations." Modelled upon the five-power declaration by the USA, U.K., France, Germany and Italy of December 12, 1932, the Political Commission of the Conference for the Reduction and Limitation of Armaments adopted the following text on March 2, 1933:

> The Governments of..., Anxious to further the cause of disarmament by increasing the spirit of mutual confidence between the nations of Europe

by means of a declaration expressly forbidding resort to force in the circumstances in which the Pact of Paris forbids resort to war, thereby solemnly reaffirm that they will not in any circumstances resort, as between themselves, to force as an instrument of national policy.

Confidence-building measures in Europe are negotiated within the East-West political-military context, which is characterized by both conflict and cooperation. NATO and Warsaw Pact nations put forward proposals with the intention of effecting changes or modifications within the existing European security order in accordance with national policies. That is power politics at play. Confidence-building measures thus form no panacea for the difficult problems of the East-West security relationship. They will not establish confidence overnight. The more meaningful and far-reaching the proposals, the more difficult they are to negotiate. In this respect CBMs are no different than other East-West arms control proposals.

If confidence-building measures are to improve security in Europe, they will have to be militarily significant. But CBMs may also serve a deeper political purpose, insofar as they can contribute to shaping a more cooperative pattern of military relations in East-West security affairs. There are clear limits as to how far cooperation can go in an area which traditionally has been marked by secrecy, antagonism and distrust, particularly when basic approaches to security and confidence-building differ markedly in East and West. Hence, building military confidence in Europe should be seen as a continuous process, taking place within the CSCE framework, which is a slow and cumbersome process, requiring agreement by all 35 states involved.

This study is limited mainly to an examination of confidence-building measures in the CSCE. It establishes a framework for thinking about military confidence-building, discusses the evolution of the concept, and concentrates attention on the current negotiations. It considers the different approaches to military confidence-building in East-West relations, the proposals put forward, the rationale behind the proposals and the objectives and goals of the participants. It also tries to analyze the kinds of contributions these measures can make to European security, as well as their inherent limitations. Finally, it assesses the likelihood of tangible results arising from the CSCE/CDE process, noting what we should expect from the CDE in its first and second stages.

II.

Military Confidence-Building:
a Conceptual Framework

The overriding difficulty in establishing even a skeletal conceptual framework for military confidence-building is reconciling the two competing approaches to confidence-building as reflected in the Stockholm Conference — an Eastern approach based mainly on declaratory political measures, and a Western approach based on measures of notification, stabilization, observation and verification. Another difficulty to be resolved involves the zone of application of the agreed measures. This makes it particularly difficult to arrive at negotiated CBMs, as the diplomatic history in this field clearly shows. The negotiation of concrete CBMs, of the kind and character now being discussed in Stockholm, has been on the diplomatic agenda for nearly three decades. During this period the position of the main alliance groupings towards military confidence-building has remained fairly constant. Indeed, one is struck by how little change there has been in both argument and philosophy in a period which has otherwise been marked by huge technological changes and developments.

The basic rationale for a confidence-building regime in Europe is the fact that the largest concentration of conventional military power in the world is located in the heart of this small continent. A large part of European military activities is shrouded in secrecy and thus gives rise to uncertainty and tension. War in Europe could break out as a result of flawed judgments or miscalculations stemming from fears of surprise attack and uncertainty about the military intentions of an adversary. Accordingly, carefully defined procedures involving information, notification, stabilization and verification to make military activities in Europe more predictable would reassure governments that those activities were routine and non-threatening.

A military confidence-building regime in Europe should primarily encompass a framework for understanding the significance of military activities and the military units involved. A pattern should be established whereby the states concerned could demonstrate that military forces in peacetime are intended only for defense and not for attack. Such a picture of normal peacetime activities would also make it easier to detect abnormal activities that could give cause for particular concern. It would then become clear whether an activity taking place during a period of tension had already been planned long in advance as a routine exercise, or instead whether it was intended as a warning or possibly as preparation for a surprise attack. In the latter case, the states concerned would be given critical warning time essential to undertake necessary precautions. Specific arrangements should also be made to ascertain whether activities are routine or threatening through the dispatch of military observers, inspection, or comparing the activity in question with data already released about it. Such a military confidence-building regime, in addition to reducing the possibilities for a military confrontation in Europe, would also reduce the possibilities for military force being used for purposes of political intimidation.

The minimum requirement for any confidence-building regime in Europe would be that it actually increases the security of the states involved, for increased confidence is very often the product of increased security, or at least the feeling of increased security. The key attributes of such a system would be greater openness (less secrecy), predictability and stability. Ultimately, the main test of a CBM regime for Europe is how well it functions in time of crisis. The measures to be adopted have to be designed with this in mind, so as to reduce possibilities for deception and increase the opportunities for confirming the peaceful intentions of ambiguous activities.

In order to be militarily significant, a CBM regime should consist of a number of concrete measures specifically aimed at neutralizing military force as an agent of change in international relations. Such measures could include obtaining early warning indicators of a possible surprise attack, establishing mechanisms of crisis management, communication and clarification, restraining the use of military force, as well as measures designed to provide information on the force structures of the participating states.

The operative elements of such a system would be measures for the exchange of information and the stabilization of military activities mainly through notification, observation and verification. It has generally been observed that such a confidence-building regime would not address the actual capabilities for war — that is, the number of troops and weapons. In fact, it is quite possible to envisage a confidence-building regime which also contains measures that operationally constrain the use of force. The challenge, though, is to develop constraint measures that affect the military capabilities of the two main alliances as well as those of neutral and non-aligned states, in equal measure.

The history of negotiating CBMs appears to bear out the proposition that the more militarily significant a confidence-building measure is, the harder it will be to negotiate. The more a measure is designed seriously to restrain capabilities, the harder it is to obtain agreement. For instance, it proved relatively easy to negotiate the "first-generation", largely voluntary CBMs contained in the 1975 Helsinki Final Act. Experience so far has shown that getting agreement on the more far-reaching measures now being discussed in the CDE will be considerably more difficult.

This is all the more true because there are differing approaches to the problem of confidence-building, especially as regards openness and access to information between East and West. The Eastern countries generally tend to downplay the importance of openness and access, and view (military) confidence-building instead as a process involving improved political relationships, which will have to precede the negotiation of concrete confidence-building measures. Moreover, the Soviet Union has consistently asserted that openness in the field of information will result in intelligence gathering which could be used for purposes of surprise attack.

Opinions differ as to whether increased openness and access will contribute to greater confidence, stability, and predictability. It may seem paradoxical that uncertainty in Western deterrence theory is considered a "good" thing ("in the uncertainty lies the deterrent"), whereas uncertainty in a CBM context is a "bad" thing. These two cases, however, are not really comparable. In peacetime and in periods of crisis, uncertainty about the intentions and activities of a possible adversary may prove to be destabilizing and lead to pre-emptive action. Nevertheless, the fact is that the Eastern countries simply do not accept the contention that more "openness" (or "transparency") will lead to greater confidence.

The counterargument to this is that confidence-building measures are designed neither to gather intelligence about the other party's force posture, nor to illuminate operational aspects of military activities. National-technical means of verification (NTM), such as reconnaissance satellites, as well as modern electronic intelligence, would most probably be up to the task of revealing indications of imminent hostile activities and aggression. The role of CBMs in providing reassurances against surprise attack lies not so much in determining the existence of specific military activities as in ascertaining the character and further clarifying the intentions related to such activity (provided that the party concerned has access to NTM information, which is not the case for all countries concerned). A CBM regime would establish the necessary political grounds for doing so, and so constitute a valuable supplement to existing national-technical means of surveillance.

Whether purely declaratory undertakings should be included in a confidence-building regime is a controversial issue. Vague and unverifiable statements of political intention have little value in concrete terms and do not per se enhance security. Declarations of intent concerning no-first-use of nuclear weapons are hardly credible unless accompanied by corresponding changes in force postures. At the same time it cannot be said in any absolute sense that declaratory statements of intent are devoid of potential for confidence-building. A statement of intent expressly prohibiting the use of military force for purposes of political intimidation might well serve such a purpose. Taking into consideration the strong political interest of the Eastern countries and the fact that the CDE operates on the basis of consensus, it appears clear that the final negotiated outcome of the CDE will have to include a combination of concrete military confidence-building measures and some "declaratory" formulations, particularly related to the non-use of force.

In which perspective, then, should the prospects for a confidence-building regime for Europe be viewed? Clearly, building the regime is a continuous and ongoing process, which is neither a panacea nor an entirely new approach to arms control. Second, confidence-building, if carried too far, may paradoxically tend to exaggerate the role played by miscalculation and misperception as causes of conflict and war. Such a simplistic approach to (military) confidence-building and conflicts does not adequately take into account the simple reality that almost all international conflicts are the result of profound clashes of national interests. Neither military confidence-building nor arms control efforts can eliminate the tension or fear which ensue from such a clash of interests, nor should they be expected to do so.

In the case of Western Europe the main security threat is the offensive military strategy of the Warsaw Pact and the forward-oriented Soviet force posture in central Europe, which in Western eyes constitutes a conventional "first-strike" capability. The Soviet concept of security underlying this force posture is detrimental to Western security interests; through the MBFR negotiations on conventional force reductions in Vienna these countries have tried, so far without success, to bring about changes in the existing Soviet force posture. No military confidence-building regime in Europe based on information, notification and stabilization measures will change that posture. It is possible, though, that such a regime could marginally raise the threshold for military aggression and thus reduce the possibilities for surprise attack. One area where a CBM regime could tangibly enhance security in Europe is crisis prevention and management.

There is, finally, the political context of military confidence-building to consider. Such a process does not take place in a political vacuum. Clearly, nations put forward proposals aimed at advancing their positions in the existing security order in Europe and attaining increased influence in the present-day distribution of power. In the CSCE context competition coexists with cooperation. Competition in the military field comes more easily than cooperation. By concentrating on military affairs, one runs the risk of highlighting those security issues on which states feel most deeply. If the essence of military confidence-building is the mutual engagement in reciprocal and cooperative measures designed to "shorten the shadow of uncertainty and fear too often on the other side of the hill" (Holst), then the participating states have a long way to go, and the whole process should be seen in a long-term perspective. In this light it can perhaps be argued that, ultimately, the context of political cooperation is the most important one, and that the arms control effect of military confidence-building comes second. One of the dilemmas of the Stockholm Conference has been precisely how to balance confidence-building measures which, according to the Madrid mandate, shall be "militarily significant" and verifiable with the generally expressed political desire of the CSCE participating states to undertake mutual East-West engagements in the military field based on reciprocity and cooperation. In other words, is there sufficient trust for militarily significant confidence-building measures?

According to the Madrid mandate the measures to be negotiated in Stockholm are both confidence- and *security*-building measures. There is a paradox inherent in this concept, not only because states have different perceptions of what constitutes confidence and security, but also because some security measures are not perceived as building confidence, and some confidence-building measures are not seen as enhancing security. There is a built-in friction in the negotiating process, which is also clearly seen in the differing approaches to the question of compliance and verification.

It is, of course, the essence of diplomacy to stress and underline the elements of common ground and not unduly emphasize divisive elements. Unfortunately, in the present world of multilateral diplomacy things do not always work out that way. If enhanced security is the objective of the Stockholm Conference, then the results in the first instance have to be militarily significant, and not only give symbolic political satisfaction. Yet the basic dilemma persists: to what extent is it possible to negotiate militarily significant confidence-building measures inside the CSCE/CDE context, based on its rather cumbersome decision-making apparatus and the accent on political cooperation?

III.

The Road to Stockholm

1. Western and Eastern Views

Confidence-building measures, especially in the military field, have generally been treated in the professional literature as a relatively new approach to regulating political-military relations between East and West. Most analyses proceed from the modest set of CBMs agreed to in the Helsinki Final Act of 1975. While some specialists have pointed to earlier CBM-type arrangements, such as the 1963 Soviet-American "Hotline" accord, the predominant tendency has been to consider developments, both political and conceptual, that have taken place since 1975. In fact, the notion of confidence-building measures goes back at least to 1955, when, in response to a Soviet-American exchange on methods of verification, the UN General Assembly urged the early adoption "of such confidence-building measures" as the exchange of military blueprints, aerial inspection, and the establishment of control posts at strategic centers.[1] One of the main obstacles to the elaboration of an effective military confidence-building regime for Europe lies in the fact that Eastern and Western approaches to military CBMs have remained essentially unchanged over the past thirty years. This should hardly be surprising, since the approaches themselves reflect conflicting and at times incompatible security and foreign-policy interests.

In sum, the NATO position, in the first instance that of the United States, has been that effective military-technical measures, specifically designed to minimize the possibility of surprise attack, should constitute the core of any comprehensive confidence-building regime. Together with this, and just as important, reliable cooperative means of verifying such arrangements would have to be worked out. As Harold Stassen, then U.S. Deputy Representative to the UN Disarmament Subcommittee, put it in 1955: "the establishment of an effective method of inspection,

---

[1]Keesing, *Disarmament Negotiations and Treaties,* Research Report 7, p. 61.

reporting and control is the first requirement for a sound agreement in relation to armaments...." Stassen went on to say:

> If there is to be an agreed suit of armaments for the major nations, the fabric of inspection must first be woven, out of which the suit may then be tailored....Let us concentrate on the factor of surprise attack, on the delivery system question, on openness concerning our military posture and potential.[2]

A main purpose of such measures, in the Western view, is to present credible information verifying the absence of feared threats. This would in particular reduce the possibility of accidents leading to pre-emptive attacks, thereby reducing the danger of attack arising out of miscalculation. Another goal has been, through the erection of adequate warning mechanisms, to provide sufficient time for the defender to effect measures of self-defense, thereby deterring the prospect of any such attack in the first place. The twin functions of an effective confidence-building regime—confirming the absence of preparations for a surprise attack and buying time for the defense—would lead, in the Western view, to a relaxation of tension. Taking into account changing circumstances and nuances of approach, the Western NATO position, first elaborated in the mid-1950s, has remained essentially the same ever since. Toward these ends the U.S. proposed in 1955, during the Geneva summit conference, mutual aerial inspection of Soviet and American territories by each other's aircraft. Such a system of "Open Skies" was to have been supplemented by the posting of ground observers in each nation for corroboration of monitored information. The proposal was rejected by the Soviet Union, for reasons described below.

The Eastern position, i.e., that of the USSR, was formulated in response to the Western approach outlined above. It has in its fundamentals remained as consistent as the Western attitude, and just as opposed to it, to this day. Where the Western NATO countries saw verification measures as an essential precondition to the discussion of military confidence-building and disarmament measures, the USSR held that the verification issue was largely a red herring, designed to deflect attention from the imperative of disarmament if not actually designed to facilitate espionage and the gathering of vital military intelligence in the Warsaw Pact states.

---

[2]U.S. Department of State, *Documents on Disarmament 1945-1959*. Vol. I (Washington, D.C.: U.S. Government Printing Office, 1960), p. 510.

Secondly, whereas Western officials saw the elaboration of specific military CBMs as the foundation for a broader relaxation of tensions, the USSR held just the opposite. "Military-technical" measures, as Soviet spokesmen called them, could not substitute for the absence of political confidence, which was the real basis for far-reaching arms control and disarmament measures. The Soviet Union has thus consistently resisted such monitoring proposals as the "Open Skies" plan, which in the Soviet view should follow rather than precede agreement on arms control and disarmament measures.

Furthermore, Soviet proposals in the CBM field have been closely integrated into the general Soviet political-military strategy toward Europe. Although the USSR has advanced proposals aimed at reducing the risk of surprise attack—especially through the exchange of military observers—in the main the Soviets have introduced far-reaching proposals involving contractual political obligations. The USSR has thus focused its attention in the confidence-building field on such broad political ("declaratory," in Western terminology) measures as a "collective security" arrangement for Europe and, when that fell through, a treaty on the non-use of force. Since the neutralization of NATO's nuclear first-use option has long been a goal of Soviet military policy, the USSR has in recent years highlighted no-first-use of nuclear weapons as a key political-military CBM. Other Soviet proposals with a similar aim, such as the establishment of nuclear weapons-free zones in Europe, have been on the Soviet policy agenda since the mid-1950s.

Thus, by the mid-1950s two main contending approaches to military confidence-building and European security had arisen, each with its own set of premises, philosophical outlook, and specific interests to defend and advance. Thirty years later the same basic distinction persists. Almost all of the intervening diplomatic and negotiating experience—whether it be President Eisenhower's "Open Skies" proposal of 1955, the Geneva Surprise Attack Conference of 1958, the similar deliberations that took place in the UN Eighteen Nation Disarmament Conference from 1962 to 1964, or the Stockholm Conference on Disarmament in Europe in 1986—has tended to reconfirm the positions staked out three decades ago.[3] The "Open Skies" proposal, and its rejection by the Soviet Union,

---

[3]See the documentation in the Appendix.

has already been mentioned. During the Geneva Surprise Attack Conference of 1958, both sides reached an impasse over the issue of the relationship between arms control and verification. Whereas the Western countries emphasized the priority of establishing an exacting system of observation and verification concerning means of surprise attack, the Soviet position stressed the importance of first banning nuclear weapons and reducing conventional forces. Discussion of verification measures could follow thereafter. The same arguments were repeated in the Eighteen Nation Disarmament Conference, held under UN auspices from 1962-1964. Though a greater appreciation for the logic of both sides' perspectives appears to have emerged from these gatherings, none of the essential positions had changed.

2. Military Confidence-Building in the 1970s

Until the signing of the Helsinki Final Act in 1975, military confidence-building measures were never formally acknowledged and given a role in European security. In the 1975 document on CBMs, the parties "recognized the need to contribute to reducing the dangers of armed conflict and of misunderstanding or miscalculation of military activities which could give rise to apprehension, particularly in a situation where the participating states lack clear and timely information about the nature of such activities." Most importantly, the parties agreed to notify major military maneuvers exceeding 25,000 troops. (For Turkey and the USSR, whose territory extends beyond Europe, prior notification need only be given of maneuvers taking place within 250 kilometers of their European frontier. This accorded the Soviet Union a privileged position inside the CSCE system.) The military provisions of the Final Act (see Appendix) also deal with the question of observers and the notification of other military maneuvers and of major military movements. These first confidence-building measures were rather modest and limited in scope. They covered a limited spectrum of military activities and were largely voluntary in character. In the CSCE follow-up meeting in Belgrade as well as in other forums, proposals were made to broaden the scope of the military confidence-building measures contained in the Final Act.

At the first UN Special Session on Disarmament in May 1978, for instance, French President Giscard d'Estaing proposed a new European Disarmament Conference, originally envisaged as a separate exercise from the CSCE but subsequently tied very closely to the CSCE process. The emphasis was on a first-stage agreement involving mandatory, verifiable and militarily significant confidence-building measures as distinct from the modest 1975 CBMs. This would be followed by a second stage dedicated to the reduction of conventional forces (nuclear issues were excluded from the conference both in the original French concept and in the modified Allied proposal). Most importantly, the zone of application for the new CBMs would be extended to the Ural mountains.

A Warsaw Pact communique of May 15, 1979 proposed a conference on military detente and an all-European security conference to achieve military detente. The Soviets had already proposed such a conference at the Belgrade CSCE follow-up meeting in 1977, envisaging it as outside the CSCE framework (and thereby avoiding the human rights issue). Soviet President Brezhnev supported the idea of such a conference in his Berlin speech of October 6, 1979, which also contained outlines for concrete military confidence-building measures in addition to long-standing Soviet proposals for such political CBMs as no-first-use of nuclear weapons, a non-aggression pact, and the proposal that neither alliance expand its current membership. Thus, well before the Stockholm conference opened on January 16, 1984, a broad range of confidence-building measures had been introduced and were well known. Among the most important of these were:

- notification of smaller maneuvers and movements with lowered thresholds, and an extended notification period (Western countries and neutral and non-aligned countries [N/NA]);
- notification of mobilization activities (France);
- notification of air maneuvers (Yugoslavia and USSR);
- notification of naval maneuvers (N/NA and Romania in Belgrade);
- notification of aggregate maneuvers exceeding 25,000 men (N/NA countries in Belgrade);
- maneuver ceiling of 40-50,000 men (USSR in Belgrade);
- forbidding multinational maneuvers near frontiers (Romania in Belgrade);
- freezing or reducing military budgets (Romania/USSR in Belgrade);
- no-first-use of nuclear weapons or military force (USSR in Belgrade);

- code of conduct and increased facilities for observers (Western countries and N/NA countries in Belgrade).

By the time of the Madrid follow-up meeting it was well known that the NATO countries, in preparing for the CDE conference mandate, would propose such confidence-building measures as observer teams, publication of annual schedules of principal military activities, exchange of military information and budgets, and the notification of mobilization activities.

The CSCE/CDE framework was not the only forum in which confidence-building measures were discussed in the context of European security. In the MBFR talks as well the focus was very much on confidence-building measures (called "associated measures" in the MBFR context). The NATO position in the CDE was strongly influenced by these associated measures, which were introduced by Western negotiators in Vienna in December 1979, and by Eastern MBFR negotiators in December 1980. Proposed Western measures included: prior notification of out-of-garrison activities and exchange of observers at such activities; ground and aerial inspection (eighteen inspections per year); declared troop entry/exit points with observers; exchange of information on manpower and structure; and non-interference with national-technical means of verification.

In several instances measures proposed by the Warsaw Pact closely paralleled those put forward by NATO. Some of the more distinctive Warsaw Pact measures included: temporary control points with observers during withdrawal period; prior notification of large (20,000 or more) exercises and troop movements; limitations (40-50,000) on military exercises; consultations in the event of doubts concerning compliance; and temporary mixed commissions to consider questions regarding implementation. The connection between the "associated" measures being discussed in MBFR and the CBMs developed within the CSCE thus appears quite clear. Both are concerned with establishing and confirming patterns of routine, non-threatening military activity, thereby enhancing confidence and security in Europe. In MBFR, however, the measures have from the start been directly linked to the actual reduction of forces.

3. The Non-Use of Force Issue

Few Soviet proposals in the field of security and disarmament have been put forward with more vigor and consistency than Soviet proposals on the non-use of force. This accords with the Soviet view that disarmament and security depend on general principles of mutual trust and relaxation of tensions, and on the necessity of improving the general political climate. In the Soviet view, the signing of a non-aggression treaty between the two main alliances has an intrinsic value in improving the international climate and building confidence. Recently, the Soviet Union has acknowledged that such a pledge should be accompanied by corresponding measures to reduce capabilities. In general, however, Soviet negotiators have always preferred to seek agreement on very broad principles, and in this sense a certain amount of ambiguity seems to have served their purpose. Such an approach has also been in line with the general Soviet approach to arms control, which has been less concerned with stability and balance than with obtaining certain security objectives—of both a political and military character—either through formal agreements or through the negotiating process itself.

The original Soviet proposal for a non-use of force treaty in the CDE was closely linked to earlier Soviet proposals for the establishment of a collective European security pact aimed at the dissolution of existing military alliances, the confirmation of the Soviet position in Eastern Europe, and according the Soviet Union a *droit de regard* in West European political-military affairs. After the integration of the two German states into the respective alliance systems, the Soviet Union dropped its call for a collective security pact, while retaining the proposal for a non-aggression pact, which essentially serves the same Soviet purposes. In addition, the non-use of force idea increasingly came to serve as a kind of Soviet "umbrella" proposal, into which other Soviet objectives or proposals have been incorporated.

Every Soviet proposal for a treaty on the non-use of force — such as those put forward at the 1954 Four Power Conference on Berlin, at the 1958 Geneva Surprise Attack Conference, and at the Stockholm Conference on Disarmament in 1985 — has included a provision for the establishment of special political and military monitoring bodies and for the convening of political and military consultations when any country party to the treaty determines that there is a danger of armed attack in Europe. The vagueness of the terms of reference, the absence of specific criteria, and the obtrusiveness of the proposed treaty's consultative mechanisms have led Western observers to conclude that such a treaty would actually go a long way toward providing the USSR with an effective veto over West European security affairs. It seems very likely, for example, that had such a procedure been set up at the time of the NATO INF deployments, the USSR would have invoked the treaty in an attempt to foil the deployments, arguing that they were a threat to peace in Europe. During the CDE sessions, for instance, Soviet negotiators, echoing their predecessors in the UN Disarmament Committee two decades earlier, stated informally that a non-use of force treaty would assist national parliaments in conducting peaceful policies, thus serving to restrain governments from conducting "aggressive" foreign policies. The form in which the principle of non-use of force has been embodied by the USSR — as a legally binding treaty with extensive political consultative mechanisms — has meant that there is little chance of negotiating such a treaty, in Stockholm or elsewhere. The link that the USSR has recently made between non-use of force and no-first-use of nuclear weapons further highlights the extent to which the proposal, like other Soviet CBM proposals, reflects a very specific Soviet political-military strategy (i.e., neutralizing NATO's policy of flexible response). In this light, the Soviet approach to the non-use of force issue highlights the sharp conflicts of interest lying behind the contending approaches to military confidence-building. The main objectives of such a treaty (as with a number of other Soviet declaratory proposals, in greater or lesser degree) appear to be:

- to establish a European security environment which would be conducive to overall Soviet political and military interests;

- to provide the Soviet Union with a *droit de regard* and leverage in West European security affairs, mainly through the treaty's consultation mechanisms, an essential part of the treaty;

- to serve as a useful instrument in influencing Western public opinion;

- to neutralize NATO's first-use option and in general weaken U.S. nuclear guarantees to Europe, while at the same time maintaining Soviet conventional force postures;

- to serve as a useful "umbrella" for other Soviet proposals in the field of security and disarmament.

4. Nuclear Disengagement Zones

There is a long history to the discussion of nuclear disengagement zones in various parts of Europe, going back to the Rapacki Plan of 1957. In general, the NATO countries have not seen the establishment of such zones as conducive to their security. Soviet reasons for proposing such zones are generally believed to be politically motivated. Through the security guarantees that such arrangements would entail, the Soviet Union would have — as in its proposed non-use of force treaty — an institutionalized *droit de regard* into European defense and security matters. The kinds of zones discussed by the Warsaw Pact countries would furthermore weaken the U.S. military presence in Europe and tend to decouple the defense of Western Europe from the United States.

The Soviet Union has also stated that it would welcome the establishment of nuclear weapons-free states, as in the Nordic case, as representing a transition towards a stance of political neutrality throughout the region. In the Nordic case, the Soviet Union has made it clear that its preference would be for a Nordic nuclear weapons-free zone consisting of countries which are already free of nuclear weapons, while excluding Soviet territory and the Baltic. From a military viewpoint, the main objective behind Soviet proposals for such zones would seem to be to neutralize NATO's nuclear option. The fact that modern technology and the extended range of modern missiles have outdated the concept of restricted geographical zones highlights the very political character of such a proposal.

In 1982 the Independent Commission on Disarmament and Security Issues proposed the establishment of a battlefield nuclear weapons-free zone in Europe, extending to a width of 150 kilometers on either side of the German border. The Soviet Union proposed to expand the zone in such way that it would include practically the whole of the Federal Republic of Germany. NATO countries have been hesitant about this idea because it would involve complex operations of verification and dual-capable systems. Nuclear battlefield systems, for instance, might be reintroduced into such a zone. Once again, broader political goals, i.e., the neutralization of NATO's nuclear-based strategy, would seem to be the object of the Soviet variant of such a zone. As long as NATO continues to pursue a strategy that does not preclude a nuclear-first use option, such proposals strike at the heart of its security concept and are therefore non-negotiable.

From an arms control viewpoint, then, the problem facing European negotiators today is very much the one before them thirty years ago. The two sides have developed mutually incompatible concepts of security in Europe. The Soviet Union argues for political measures, whereas the West stresses the necessity for military-technical measures. The West has held that CBMs have an intrinsic value by reducing the danger of surprise attack and making for increased stability through greater openness and less uncertainty, thereby reducing the chances for the outbreak of an accidental or unintended war through misperception and miscalculation. The Soviet Union has displayed an interest in measures which could constrain allied military exercises (especially those involving U.S. reinforcements to Europe) and has eventually come to accept prenotification of certain military activities and exchanges of military observers. The Soviets have also qualified their opposition to inspection measures, as they are part of specific arms control and disarmament agreements. Nevertheless, the Soviet Union has continued to be generally hostile to measures of information and inspection/verification, which they have contended are tantamount to legalizing espionage and intelligence gathering to the detriment of Soviet security. It is very difficult at best to reconcile these two contradictory concepts of arms control, that is to say, of contradictory concepts of national and alliance security. Prospects for the negotiation and successful implementation of a military confidence-building regime in Europe depend very much on whether these two concepts of security, and the conflicting interests that lie behind them, can be even partially resolved.

IV.

The Conference on Confidence- and Security-Building Measures and Disarmament in Europe: Proposals, Objectives, Issues

The Conference on Confidence- and Security-Building Measures and Disarmament in Europe (CDE) opened in Stockholm on January 17, 1984. In contrast to the beginning of the CSCE in the early 1970s, the Stockholm Conference opened under rather adverse international conditions, with superpower relations at their lowest ebb since the cold war. The U.S.-Soviet relationship clearly put its mark on the Stockholm Conference. Parties to the conference at first concentrated on the most contentious and sensitive issues and advanced proposals which, taking past experience into consideration, were difficult to negotiate. With the impasse or collapse of other East-West negotiating forums, the Stockholm Conference tended to be overburdened with largely extraneous issues and was treated by the USSR as a propaganda platform for launching proposals and declarations mainly designed to influence Western public opinion.

The fundamentally differing approaches of the main parties to the Stockholm Conference have their background not only in different perceptions and approaches to security and arms control, but also in different interests and objectives regarding the distribution of power within the existing European security order. The proposals advanced by the parties reflect long-standing national policy objectives and priorities. In this perspective the NATO proposals are the more static and status quo oriented, whereas the Soviet/WTO proposals are more designed to change and influence the prevailing security pattern.

In practical terms East and West differ in the CDE on the following key issues: (1) the *character* of the confidence- and security-building measures to be adopted; (2) the *scope* of the CSBMs (constraint measures, naval and air activities, verification and observation); (3) the *extent* of the CDE zone; and (4) the issue of verification. All of these issues are connected with conflicting interpretations of the Madrid mandate for the Stockholm Conference.

1. The Mandate

At the Stockholm Conference both NATO and the Warsaw Pact, as well as the neutral and non-aligned countries, adopted positions consistent with their earlier approaches to military confidence-building. The central document for the Conference is the Conference mandate, which was painstakingly negotiated for over three years at the CSCE follow-up meeting in Madrid from 1980 to 1983 (see Appendix).

The Madrid mandate states very clearly that the Stockholm Conference is part of the CSCE process. The aim of the Conference is "to undertake, in stages, new, effective and concrete actions designed to make progress in strengthening confidence and security and in achieving disarmament so as to give effect and expression to the duty of states to refrain from the threat or use of force in their mutual relations." According to the mandate, the conference will begin a process whose first stage is to be devoted to the negotiation and adoption of a set of complementary confidence- and security-building measures designed to reduce the risk of military confrontation in Europe. These confidence- and security-building measures will cover the whole of Europe as well as the adjoining sea area and air space. They will be of military significance, politically binding, and provided with adequate forms of verification. In a footnote, the mandate stipulates that as far as the adjoining sea area and air space is concerned, the measures will be applicable to the military activities of all participating states whenever these activities affect security in Europe. As regards follow-up mechanisms, the Madrid mandate states that the November 1986 CSCE follow-up meeting in Vienna will assess the progress achieved during the first stage of the CDE. A further CSCE follow-up meeting will consider the question of supplementing the present mandate for the next stage of the conference in light both of the results achieved in the first stage of the Conference and of other relevant negotiations on security and disarmament affecting Europe.

The most difficult problem facing negotiators in Madrid was the extension of the CSBM zone of application, with the Soviet Union long resisting the proposal to include the whole of Europe within the zone of application. Agreement finally became possible when the Soviet Union accepted the inclusion of the European part of the USSR in the zone of application, on the stated condition that the zone be expanded correspondingly in the West. The Soviet position, however, did not prevail, and the Madrid mandate makes clear that the Stockholm Conference is predominantly concerned with land-based military activities in Europe, and that independent naval and air activities are not included.

2. The Proposals

On the Western side, the overall objective was to give practical expression to the principle of the non-use of force. The NATO packet, tabled in January 1984, called for:

1) exchange of detailed information on military force structures;

2) exchange of forecasts of military activities;

3) 45-day pre-notification of the following out-of-garrison land activities:

- movement of one or more ground force divisions or equivalent formations, or 6,000 or more ground troops not organized into a division;

- mobilization activities, involving 25,000 or more troops;

- amphibious activities, involving three or more battalions, or 3,000 amphibious troops carrying out a landing in the CDE zone of application.

4) observation of military activities through observers;

5) compliance and verification through national-technical means and inspection (two inspections annually from the ground or by air);

6) development of means of communication.[4]

The Western approach is based on encouraging greater openness and predictability in military activities so as to reduce the risk of surprise attack or the outbreak of war due to misunderstanding or miscalculation.

---

[4]See the text of the NATO proposal tabled in Stockholm, Conference on Security and Cooperation in Europe/Stockholm Conference, Stockholm, January 24, 1984 (in Appendix). Hereafter referred to as CSCE/SC.

In the NATO view the proposed measures are complementary and inter-linked. In June 1984, Ambassador James Goodby presented the Western rationale in the following way:

> These measures are mutually reinforcing. Their objective is to reduce ten-sions, to promote common understanding among all participants, and to diminish the danger of armed conflict arising from misunderstanding or mis-calculation. The focus is on preventing a sequence of events which has all too often led to war on the continent of Europe: the incident, military move-ment or political event which is misunderstood, with misunderstanding lead-ing to suspicion, reaction, escalation, and perhaps confrontation and conflict.[5]

The six points of the Western proposal can be implemented easily with a minimum of intrusion or alteration of normal, non-threatening military activity. The process would work approximately as follows:

A context of basic information is established through Measure 1, near the end of each year. Much of the information which would be exchanged is already available to the CSCE states through other means. At the same time, under Measure 2, a state would advise the other partici-pants of its planned military activities during the next calendar year. Be-cause modern training and rotational activities are so complex and planned a year or more in advance, military forces routinely develop this kind of information.

Measure 3, on pre-notification, then provides more detail, and also a cross-check on the forecast. If a state should notify under Measure 3 an activity not previously forecast, other countries could demand an explan-ation of the apparent anomaly. A nation with aggressive intent would then be raising an alarm against itself if it announced an exercise which it had not forecast, and, of course, this alarm would sound even louder if a coun-try failed either to forecast or to notify forty-five days in advance of the event. The measures are thus self-enforcing.

The observers called for in Measure 4 serve to verify that activities are in fact taking place as advertised. There may be occasions, however, when one state sees, or thinks it sees, an activity that has not been notified but should have been. In such a case, under Measure 5, suspicions can be alleviated or confirmed by asking for verification, either by direct observation, if necessary, or by some other appropriate means. The

---

[5]"Security for Europe," *NATO Review,* June 1984.

communications network provided by Measure 6 could be utilized to seek further information on a potentially destabilizing event.

These measures would not in themselves prevent war. They could not prevent a determined state from using force for political intimidation. But they could make unwanted confrontation less likely and raise the political cost of using force to intimidate. By establishing a pattern of routine activities, anomalies would stand out clearly. Governments would know with reasonable certainty what was supposed to happen. If a departure from the routine pattern occurred, they would have time either to clarify the situation before political tensions escalated or take counteraction against a real threat. Eventually, the result should be an increase in confidence and stability among the participating countries.

The Soviet Union stressed the importance of rather broad and general political proposals, most of which were well known from earlier negotiations. These included:

- a commitment by nuclear powers not to be the first to use nuclear weapons;
- the conclusion of a treaty on the non-use of military force;
- a freeze and reduction of military spending, in percentage points or absolute terms;
- ridding Europe of chemical weapons — as a first step, the non-stationing of chemical weapons in areas where presently there are none;
- creation of nuclear weapons-free zones in various parts of Europe;
- the elaboration of additional Helsinki-type CBMs, such as:
  i   putting a ceiling of 40,000 men on military maneuvers;
  ii   prior notification of major military maneuvers of ground troops, air and naval forces, conducted independently or jointly in Europe and the adjoining sea area and air space (military maneuver of ground troops involving 20,000 men would be notified 30 days in advance);
  iii prior notification of major movements and transfers with the same specification as above;
  iv development of the existing practice of inviting observers from other participating states to attend major military maneuvers.[6]

---

[6]For the text of the Soviet proposal, see CSCE/SC.4, Stockholm, May 8, 1984 (in Appendix).

In early 1985 the Soviet Union tabled its basic provisions for a treaty on the non-use of force and the maintenance of peaceful relations.[7] In addition to the central position proscribing the use of military force, the Soviet draft aimed at stopping the U.S. Strategic Defense Initiative and called for the consideration of measures to prevent surprise attack. In keeping with its traditional approach to the non-use of force issue, the Soviets stipulated that in the event of a risk of war and the use of military force the parties to the treaty would hold urgent consultations, seek clarification and provide one another with necessary information.

The basic Soviet rationale for putting forward proposals on no-first-use and a treaty for non-use of force in the CDE was that the dramatically deteriorating political and military situation in Europe necessitated the adoption of far-reaching and drastic political measures to halt the drift towards war. In the present situation it would not suffice to concentrate on or give priority to Western "military-technical" measures, which the Soviets described as trivial and at the same time as constituting a sinister plot to elicit sensitive military information. (Indeed, the alleged connection between the Pershing II deployments and Western information proposals as a means of gathering "targeting intelligence" was quickly established by the Soviets in Stockholm.)* While the Soviets did not exclude "military-technical" measures from the Stockholm agenda, and displayed an interest in measures which could constrain Western maneuvers, the Soviets complained that the Western approach excluded from the scope of the CSBMs naval and air forces which were relevant to the European security situation.

As usual in the CSCE process, the neutral and the non-aligned countries also put forward proposals. While the general orientation of the

---

[7]For the text, see CSCE/SC.6, January 29, 1985 (in Appendix).

*This echoed earlier Soviet behavior in the negotiations conducted in the 1960s inside the Eighteen Nation Disarmament Conference, where the Soviet negotiator, Semyon Tsarapkin, linked the question of notification and information/observation to the U.S. Polaris submarines then being introduced, and stated that a war might come about "not by accident, miscalculation or failure of communication, but through premeditated action taken by the Polaris submarines." In the MBFR negotiations, as late as 1985/1986 the Soviets established the same link between the exchange of information proposal and Western targeting policies.

N/NA proposals approached the NATO proposals, the N/NA countries also included proposals for constraining military activities. The more distinctive N/NA proposals included:

- ceilings for forces engaged in major military maneuvers carried out close to each other in time and space;
- constraints on the deployment of military units and/or equipment of vital importance for sustaining offensive operations;
- arrangements for dealing with information, notification and rapid exchange of views with regard to the measures adopted.[8]

While far from specific on parameters and thresholds, the N/NA proposals nevertheless indicated that these should be substantially improved as compared to those laid down in the Final Act. On the non-use of force issue the N/NA proposal limited itself to stating that concrete confidence- and security-building measures would give effect and expression to the duty of states to refrain from the threat or use of force, and could create conditions for considering an appropriate reaffirmation of the non-use of force obligation. This approach was very close to that of the NATO countries.

The Romanian proposal was very much in line with earlier Romanian proposals in the CSCE and reflected a concern to limit very specific threats to Romanian national security. The Romanian proposals thus included limitation of armed forces participating in military maneuvers to 40-50,000 men, renunciation of multinational military maneuvers within a zone along each side of the border, creation along the borders between states of security zones, prohibition of certain kinds of maneuvers and naval and air activities, and the establishment of a crisis management system. The Romanian proposal was closer to the position of its Warsaw Pact allies in calling for the conclusion of an all-European treaty on the non-use of force, establishment of nuclear weapons-free zones or corridors in Europe, and freezing military expenditures at 1984 levels.[9]

---

[8]See CSCE/SC.3, Stockholm, March 9, 1984 as well as the more recent CSCE/SC.7, Stockholm, November 15, 1985 (in Appendix).

[9]For text, see CSCE/SC.2, Stockholm, January 25, 1984 (in Appendix).

3. The Issues and Objectives

(a) *The Character of the CSBMs*

The NATO countries claim that their proposals for CSBMs are in full accordance with the provisions of the Madrid mandate for the Conference (see above, pp. 33-35). The Western approach, therefore, is to concentrate on specific, verifiable and militarily significant CSBMs and in this way give effect and concrete expression to the principle of the non-use of force. The NATO countries maintain that most of the Soviet proposals either are not in accordance with the mandate—which stipulates that the CSBMs negotiated at Stockholm are to deal with conventional arms issues—or should be negotiated in other forums. This applies to Soviet proposals on the no-first-use issue, nuclear-free zones, chemical weapons and the freezing/reduction of military budgets. This leaves only the Soviet proposals for concrete CSBMs and the non-use of force treaty, where the NATO countries are willing to discuss certain aspects of principle, though not their embodiment in treaty form.

The Soviet and Eastern countries countered with the argument that the Madrid mandate did not explicitly prohibit the consideration of nuclear issues. The nuclear issue, in the Warsaw Pact view, is one of the most important issues threatening the European security situation, and is therefore implicitly subsumed under the mandate's stipulation that the adopted measures be "designed to reduce the risk of military confrontation in Europe." This interpretation was rejected by the NATO countries.

On no other issue has the discussion at the Stockholm Conference been so heated as on the Soviet proposal for a treaty on the non-use of force. The Soviet rationale for putting forward the treaty proposal has been dealt with in the previous section (pp.27-28). The NATO countries advanced a number of arguments of both a formal and substantive character against the Soviet idea. In general, the Western countries considered the measure to be a declaratory, and therefore unverifiable statement of intent rather than the effective expression of the principle of the non-use of force stipulated in the mandate.

One of the main Western objections to the treaty proposal was directed against the incorporation of the no-first-use clause as one of the central provisions of the proposed treaty. This provision was evidently directed against NATO force postures and the flexible response doctrine of the NATO alliance. NATO countries were not willing to isolate the nuclear issue from conventional military issues. Nuclear weapons had been incorporated into Western defense because of the imbalance in conventional forces, and on several occasions NATO had affirmed "that none of our weapons will ever be used except in response to attack."[10] Removing nuclear weapons from the NATO defense would also remove a considerable part of deterrence and thereby reduce the risks faced by a potential aggressor. By banning one special category of weapons, one should not leave Europe open to the possibility of a conventional war, which might well escalate into a nuclear war. According to the Western view, the non-use of force principle should apply as a basic obligation not to use *any* kind of force. In military terms it was argued that a pledge not to use nuclear weapons first had to be seen in connection with the force posture question. The present force postures, which in NATO's view accord a considerable conventional advantage to the Warsaw Pact, would invalidate such a pledge. The basic treaty provisions on international sea, air and space communication and the provisions that the treaty would cover all the territories of the parties to the treaty as well as their military and civilian personnel, naval, air- and space-craft and other facilities, considerably broadened the geographic scope of the CDE zone of application. Nor could the NATO countries accept the rather sweeping statements in the treaty concerning space weapons and nuclear and conventional disarmament, which were imprecise and expanded the scope of the mandate. In short, the NATO countries did not accept that the wording and the contents of the basic provisions gave concrete "effect and expression to the duty of States to refrain from the threat or use of force in their mutual relations."

The position of the NATO countries, however, does not mean that these countries will not consider the non-use of force principle in an appropriate form in Stockholm. After originally having taken a rather restricted position on the issue at the Stockholm Conference, President Reagan, in his Dublin speech on June 4, 1984, declared: "If discussions on reaffirming the principle not to use force, a principle in which we believe so deeply, will bring the Soviet Union to negotiate agreements which will give concrete new meaning to that principle, we will gladly enter into such discussions." During subsequent talks in Stockholm it

---

[10]Bonn Declaration of June 10, 1982. Text in *Europa Archiv. Dokumente. 1982* (Bonn: Verlag fuer Internationale Politik, 1982), pp. D342-D346.

has become clear that the final results will have to include some wording on the non-use of force principle. The NATO countries continue to believe, though, that even while there will be a parallel treatment of the non-use of force issue and concrete CSBMs, the main objective of the Conference is to elaborate concrete confidence- and security-building measures. In other words, the principle of the non-use of force must not simply be reaffirmed but substantiated through new measures.

(b) *The Scope of the Measures*

Whereas the NATO proposals do not contain any measures constraining military capabilities (constraint measures), such measures are common to both the N/NA proposals and the Soviet/WTO proposals. Furthermore, the latter also contain proposals for the notification of (independent) naval and air activities. In the field of compliance and verification as well there are important differences between the main groups, with the NATO countries proposing a detailed inspection and observation regime, and the Soviets being on the whole rather reticent on this matter.

The NATO countries are not in principle opposed to constraint measures, but feel that such measures will have to be looked at quite carefully in view of the asymmetry of force postures, so that these measures do not unduly hurt the military interests of one party. On the NATO side there is a feeling that the constraint proposals put forward by the N/NA countries tend to constrain NATO military activities, while leaving Warsaw Pact activities in the main unaffected. The NATO countries also argue that their own proposals will, if implemented, have a considerable constraining effect on military activities.

The N/NA and Warsaw Pact countries contend that information and notification measures are not sufficient for a CSBM regime, and that such a regime also will have to constrain military capabilities. Some N/NA countries also argue that these measures will ease the transition to the disarmament stage of the CDE. Politically, this is the most important argument for including constraint measures in Stockholm. In general, the constraint measures put forward in Stockholm can be grouped in the following way:

- constraints on military activities and equipment (ceilings on troops participating in movements and maneuvers);
- constraints on the number of troops and equipment in certain (border) areas;

• establishment of nuclear/chemical weapons-free zones and corridors.

From a NATO military viewpoint, the effect of the proposed constraint measures would seem to be greater on the NATO alliance, and to a certain extent on the various N/NA countries, than on Warsaw Pact countries. This would appear to be the case with respect to reinforcements, forward defense and overall training flexibility and opportunities — mainly as a consequence of the geographical asymmetry of the two alliances, differences in force structures and postures, and numbers of troops.

As regards the maneuver ceilings, it should be noted that the *lower* the threshold parameter, the greater the disadvantage to the NATO alliance. In general NATO holds more large-scale military exercises than the Warsaw Pact, which apparently adheres to an altogether different exercise pattern, involving a much more limited number of troops. The difference in exercise patterns is due to NATO's requirement to reinforce Europe from overseas, the greater number of allies participating in such exercises, as well as the restricted number of suitable training areas in Western Europe. A maneuver ceiling would thus inhibit Alliance flexibility in planning and executing the training of major formations. It can also be argued that a lower ceiling would impede NATO's reinforcement requirements without affecting the normal pattern of Warsaw Pact training and capability for maneuver. However, an appropriate ceiling under certain conditions may be marginally helpful in an impending surprise attack situation and restrain capabilities for applying military force for political intimidation.

From the NATO military viewpoint, the proposal to put a ceiling on the forces engaged in maneuvers carried out close to each other in time and space would be even more detrimental, and would also be considerably more difficult to verify. Correspondingly, proposals which limit amphibious, airborne or air-mobile operations would impede Allied reinforcement operations. As far as proposals for constraints on equipment are concerned, the main problem would seem to be how to exclude equipment which would be necessary for a credible defense posture while including equipment which might constrain offensive capabilities. This would, of course, activate the old dilemma of how to differentiate between offensive and defensive military equipment and highlights the importance of maintaining *self*-confidence in any CSBM regime.

Though the question of constraint measures is a complex one, possibilities exist for including constraint measures in the final negotiated outcome. Such measures, however, must not work to the detriment of the security interests of one party to the regime. Among the possibilities which should be explored, the following might be considered:

i) A Ceiling on Major Maneuvers

A ceiling of 40,000 men has already been proposed by the Warsaw Pact countries. Such a low ceiling is unacceptable to the NATO countries inasmuch as Warsaw Pact exercise activities would remain unaffected whereas NATO activities would be very effectively constrained. Both sides should explore whether a higher numerical parameter might be possible which might inhibit or constrain capabilities for the reinforcement of forces prior to a surprise attack or inhibit the use of military force for political intimidation during a crisis situation. Correspondingly, the negotiators might put a ceiling on the total number of divisions out of garrison at the same time. A third possibility would be to apply a ceiling on all military land-based activities which are not included in the annual calendar of military activities notifiable in advance.

ii) Constraints on the Deployment of Offensive Equipment or Material

The main problem with this proposal would be how to differentiate between offensive and defensive equipment, as well as problems associated with compliance and verification. It has been argued that a prohibition on the storage of heavy bridge-building equipment in forward areas would severely curtail Warsaw Pact capabilities for carrying out a large-scale attack. It has also been contended, however, that the defender might need such equipment for possible withdrawal operations. In theory, other constraint measures might also be studied. In practice, these probably would not prove easily negotiable, taking into consideration the different force postures of both sides and the wish of each not to seriously curtail its military capabilities. Very likely, any constraint measures negotiated during the first stage of the CDE will be of rather modest military significance. Opportunities exist, however, for taking up this matter at the second stage of the CDE.

(c) *Extent of the CDE Zone*

Disagreement has persisted in Stockholm on the inclusion of "independent" naval and air activities, with the Soviet Union interested in measures that would affect U.S. and NATO naval activities in the Atlantic and Mediterranean as well as the dispatch of the Rapid Deployment Force and its transfer via Europe. NATO holds that this question has already been resolved through the functional approach outlined in the mandate, which includes military activities in the sea and air space adjoining* Europe "whenever these activities affect security in Europe as well as constitute a part of activities taking place within the whole of Europe...." That is, independent naval and air activities are excluded from the scope of the mandate. On the other hand, certain naval air activities which are directly linked to ongoing land-based European military activities and which affect European security are notifiable under the mandate. As an example one may point to Norwegian notifications of the "Team Work 84" and "Avalanche Express" exercises in 1984, which contained significant naval components, as examples of how the Madrid mandate can be applied in this context. Operations that lie outside the specific framework of the mandate, such as independent air and naval maneuvers in the North Atlantic, are not to be included.[11]

(d) *The Verification Issue*

East and West have also advanced different proposals regarding the issue of compliance and verification in Stockholm. The Madrid mandate stipulates that the Stockholm CSBMs "will be of military significance and politically binding and will be provided with adequate forms of verification which will correspond to their content." N/NA and Soviet/Warsaw

---

*The term "adjoining" is understood to signify the territorial waters of the states involved.

[11]Interestingly, in Subcommittee C of the CSCE in July 1975, the Soviet delegation declared that "it is of the same point of view" as the U.S. that provisions for prior notification of maneuvers "should not be considered to apply to independent naval maneuvers, independent air maneuvers, or maneuvers involving only naval and air forces operating together." *CSCE Documents,* Phase II, Journal no. 246, July 19, 1975, Subcommittee C. Against the background of the very heavy Soviet naval build-up over the last 10 years and more, the expressed Soviet interest in including independent naval activities gives rise to certain questions. It cannot be ruled out that the Soviet negotiating position in Stockholm is caused by tactical considerations, i.e., to expand the zone of application towards the West.

Pact proposals in Stockholm have limited themselves to quoting the Madrid mandate provisions on verification, whereas the NATO countries have come up with very specific proposals.

Traditionally, U.S. insistence on strict verification procedures has been regarded by the Soviets as either "the Philistine side of arms control" and unrealistic or as merely representing a "tactic of obfuscating the substance of negotiations and torpedoing talks by exaggerated demands concerning control."[12] Any American reference to the inadequacy of verification procedures is therefore criticized as "false and hypocritical."[13] In addition, Soviet spokesmen fear that the United States puts so much emphasis on verification in the erroneous belief that this is the Soviet Union's "weak point" or, worse, that it merely provides an opportunity for spying on the Soviet Union. "Control becomes legalized espionage," according to one Soviet source, "the moment that its scope, the competence of controlling bodies, the methods of inspection and so on go beyond what is actually necessary to verify agreed disarmament measures."[14]

In practice, however, Soviet opposition to inspection and verification has never been quite as adamant as suggested in the previous passages. The Bulganin proposals of 1955 specifically referred to the stationing of inspectors at certain key locations in order to supervise and ascertain the character of certain military activities, even though these inspectors would not be given unrestricted freedom of movement and access. Furthermore, in a series of international treaties and negotiations the Soviet have accepted requirements for on-site inspection and verification. In 1983 the USSR, in the UN Committee on Disarmament, accepted the requirement for on-site inspection in connection with the destruction of declared stocks of chemical weapons. Following an agreement with the International Atomic Energy Agency (IAEA) in 1985, the Soviet Union now allows IAEA inspection of two of its civilian nuclear reactors. In the 1976 Peaceful Nuclear Explosions agreement between the U.S. and the USSR, on-site inspection is called for. Likewise, some Soviet proposals for Associated Measures in MBFR seem to take into account the need for inspection. Recent statements by Soviet General Secretary

---

[12]Daniel Frei, *Assumptions and Perceptions in Disarmament* (New York: UNIDAR, 1984), p. 70, quoting Georgi Arbatov and Viktor Israelyan, respectively.

[13]*Ibid.*

[14]*Ibid.*

Mikhail Gorbachev indicate that, under certain circumstances, the Soviet Union would be prepared to undertake quite far-reaching measures of international verification, including on-site inspection.[15] This seemed to be the case particularly with his January 15, 1986 statement, which explicitly acknowledged the need for on-site inspection. At the same time, however, it has to be stated that until now this apparent flexibility has not been followed up by Soviet negotiators in either the Stockholm Conference or the Vienna force-reduction talks.

That being said, however, the Soviet Union has never accepted inspection and verification as an arms control measure in its own right but only in close relation to specific measures of arms control and disarmament. It is also clear that the Soviet Union will be opposed to far-ranging and comprehensive proposals in the field of verification and inspection. Traditionally, the Soviet Union has judged inspection/verification measures and proposals in connection with how important the related disarmament/arms control proposals have been for the Soviet Union both militarily and politically. The more important these have been for the Soviet Union, the more the Soviet Union has been willing to give in the field of inspection and verification. Taking into consideration the fact that the Soviet Union has traditionally displayed a rather negative attitude towards most military confidence-building measures, it should not be expected that it will be very forthcoming regarding inspection and verification arrangements related to a future CSBM regime.

4. The Elements of a Negotiated Agreement in Stockholm

The basic prerequisite for any arms control agreement is that the parties involved share a common interest in such an agreement, for political or military reasons, or both. The elements of such a common ground in Stockholm are far from self-evident. The two main parties have essentially conflicting approaches to security issues, as witnessed by their main CSBM proposals. The NATO proposals contain elements which are clearly anathema to the Soviet/Warsaw Pact side, whereas the latter's proposals are equally unacceptable to the West. The basic Soviets objections to Western proposals are that they will act to the detriment

---

[15]See *Statement by Mikhail Gorbachev, General Secretary of the CPSU Central Committee* (Moscow: Novosti, 1986), pp. 7, 11-12.

of Soviet security interests and, in excluding certain naval activities, that they violate the principle of "equal security".* The main difficulty in Stockholm has been to strike a balance between "political-declaratory" proposals, constraint proposals, and CSBMs directed mainly towards information, notification and stabilization. Realistically, it must be expected that the final results will be rather limited and modest.

Nevertheless, all parties have expressed an interest in notification measures and the exchange of observers. It is to be expected that the new notification measures will lower the present threshold of 25,000 men. (The NATO proposal is one division or 6,000 men, the Soviet proposal 20,000 men.) It is also probable that the notification time will be increased from its present twenty-one days. It can also be expected that working conditions for military observers will be somewhat improved and that means of communication will be established whereby the participating states can handle the flow of information required by agreed CSBMs and for crisis management.

Agreement on notification measures, however, presupposes that the parties agree to exclude independent naval activities. Even if General Secretary Gorbachev in his January 15, 1986 statement signaled Soviet readiness to postpone this issue to the next stage in the CDE negotiations, the issue remains unresolved in Stockholm. Apart from these elements it is very hard to foresee the final outcome, taking into consideration Soviet opposition to information measures, as well as apparent Soviet reluctance to accept compliance and verification/inspection measures. Absent an agreement on exchange of military information regarding force structures, it will be difficult to ascertain the importance and significance of prenotified military activities. In addition, an agreed data base is also very important for observation and inspection purposes. Such a standard is very important. As regards verification, which is indispensable to any arms control agreement, an improved regime for military observers would enhance the possibilities for verification. Certain provisions for on-site inspection would also appear necessary, especially in connection with crisis management. The Soviets, however, still oppose giving information about the peacetime location of their forces. As regards verification,

---

*Here lies one of the paradoxes of the Stockholm Conference. The extension of the geographic zone, a major achievement at Madrid, serves to limit the kind of militarily significant CSBMs which the Soviet Union will accept to apply on its own territory.

they seem to maintain their position that national-technical means, in connection with a consulting mechanism, will suffice.

The issue of constraint measures will be difficult to negotiate, particularly because of differences in force postures, training patterns, geography and alliance composition. To a certain extent it can be argued that the NATO proposal to exchange annual forecasts of military activities could have a constraining effect, at least in staging military activities for the purpose of political intimidation. Under General Secretary Gorbachev the Soviets have now accepted the idea of such an annual calendar. The question of additional constraints on manpower ceilings should be looked into. It does not seem realistic, however, to expect that the CDE in its first stage will be able to negotiate other constraint proposals in the area of deployment or equipment.

The wording of the mandate is clear on the exclusion of independent naval and air activities. It should be possible, though, to include in a notification regime such activities which are functionally connected to ongoing land-based activities notifiable in advance.

It should also be possible to reaffirm the principle of the non-use of force in an appropriate manner. The difficulty lies in the effort by the Soviet Union to link non-use of force to other, highly controversial issues, such as no-first-use and the establishment of formal East-West consultation mechanisms for the discussion of problems of European security.

Finally, on nuclear issues, it is difficult to envisage how any final document from Stockholm can contain agreed language on nuclear weapons-free zones/corridors or the no-first-use issue. If other aspects of nuclear policy were to be included, it would certainly be possible to find agreed language in existing Soviet-American bilateral treaties.

To sum up, one can identify a range of possible outcomes from the Stockholm negotiations:

1) A "mini-packet" concentrating on notification, observation and the reaffirmation of the non-use of force principle. On notification, the Soviet Union would have to clarify if it can accept the "out of garrison"concept, which it thinks is too intrusive, or if it will insist on maintaining the Helsinki distinction between movements and maneuvers.

2) The minipacket solution, plus elements of information/verification and communication. The Soviets have not accepted information and verification as independent measures. It may prove possible, however, to arrive at a compromise solution by providing military information in other measures, for example, tying it to the annual calender and/or notification measures. It is more doubtful whether a compromise on verification is possible.

3) A balanced packet which will amount to the above (2) plus constraint measures. It does not seem likely, however, that the CDE in its first stage will manage to agree on any constraint measures.

V.

Is There a Future for Military Confidence-Building in Europe?

The confidence-building process in Europe is not confined to the framework of the CSCE/CDE. States may choose unilaterally to organize their military activities in a way that is non-provocative to their neighbors in sensitive areas. In Norwegian security and defense policy there exists a set of voluntary, self-imposed restrictions whose primary function is to display a peacetime pattern of non-hostile intentions based on predictability and stability by exercising restraint and inviting other states to show restraint. These measures include prohibitions against deploying foreign troops in time of peace, restrictions on allied military maneuvers in the northern parts of Norway, and restrictions on allied naval and air movements in northern territories. The NATO decision to withdraw 2,400 tactical nuclear weapons from Europe is another example of a unilateral confidence-building measure. It is indeed arguable that the greatest potential in military confidence-building in Europe lies precisely in unilateral national capabilities for policy-making in the field of defense policy and force postures. The immediate question, however, lies in the military and political significance of negotiated measures in Europe. The CSBMs to emerge from the CDE, after all, are supposed to be "militarily significant", in contrast to the predominantly political and psychological purpose of the Helsinki CBMs. How, then, can they actually contribute to increasing European security?

None of the CSBMs coming out of the first stage of the CDE conference can realistically be expected to reduce or blunt in any fundamental way the main obstacle to European military detente, which remains the offensive strategy and corresponding force posture of the Warsaw Pact forces in central Europe. The forward positioning and capabilities of these forces for a first-strike offensive constitute the greatest existing threat to European military stability. While CSBMs have a definite role to play in stabilizing the situation, it would be wrong to expect CSBMs to accomplish too much in this respect. CSBMs cannot change the European security situation or the nature of superpower rivalry. On the other hand, CSBMs can enhance European security and stability in marginal ways. Noting the size of the stakes involved, even a search for marginal improvements is something to be encouraged.

1. CSBMs Seeking to Build Confidence Through Greater Openness

This is in many ways the classical CBM philosphy, as imbedded in the Helsinki Final Act. The argument is still convincing. Military activities in Europe are largely shrouded in secrecy, which gives rise to anxieties that breed insecurity. Greater openness, in this view, will reduce fears. "Traffic rules" for the normal military pattern of activities in Europe will convey intentions of non-hostility, and will make anomalies stand out, giving time for preparations or clarifications and thus contributing to greater stability and predictability. Such traffic rules would also probably be marginally helpful in inhibiting the use of military force for purposes of political intimidation. Moreover, such a reciprocal pattern could induce the participants to broaden the platform for common endeavors and expand the CSBM regime. It would condition the participants to further cooperation, and establish the necessary political foundation for doing so.

In short, carefully negotiated and implemented CSBMs could serve as a useful foundation for limited East-West cooperation in selected military activities, creating a platform which hopefully could develop further. Though the measures would have military significance, they would mainly operate on the political and psychological level and serve to generate confidence in time of peace. The basic test of whether any CSBM regime works, however, will come in times of crisis, and the measures should be designed with this objective in mind.

The argument against such CSBMs is that there is a danger of over-institutionalizing the system. If the objective is to enhance the general level of confidence, that could be met through changes in political relations and the international atmosphere. This would parallel discussion going on in other arms control and disarmament forums, where it is sometimes stated, particularly by Western negotiators, that soldiers and weapons are only symptoms of underlying tensions and clashes of national interest, and that disarmament will only be possible when the underlying political conflicts are resolved or ameliorated.

2. Surprise-Attack CSBMs

The question of surprise attack has been a recurrent subject in arms control talks. Whether CSBMs can effectively reduce possibilities for a surprise attack is a disputed question. Most students of CSBMs tend to believe that no single CSBM could by itself effectively reduce the risk of a surprise attack, though some have argued it may have a marginal impact. It is probably correct that with the existing state of surveillance technology CSBMs are not necessary for the detection of surprise attack preparations and prevention.

Western military commentators have pointed to a number of activities which might indicate Soviet preparations for a surprise attack. These include: alerts and dispersal of forces; intensified reconnaissance efforts, such as increased launchings of intelligence satellites; intensified communications patterns, including changes in command and control arrangements; and the mobilization of reserves. Most specialists agree that, even though these measures may be accompanied by elaborate deception campaigns, national-technical means of intelligence would be able to detect most of them. The difficulty lies in determining whether the activities detected constitute actual preparations for a surprise attack or a political display of force, and in marshaling the political will to take appropriate countermeasures. As Richard Betts notes, "[W]arning," though necessary, "is a secondary element in the problem of surprise attack...; political and psychological impediments are primary."[16]

It has been pointed out that the reinforcement and strengthening of Soviet forces in central Europe have aggravated NATO vulnerability to a surprise attack situation. Increases in the number of tanks and artillery, a strengthening of tactical aviation forces and a modernization of theater nuclear forces have contributed to increasing Soviet capabilities for an unreinforced attack. Steven L. Canby offers the following analysis:

> Presently Soviet levels are sufficient to launch an unreinforced attack; even
> fewer troops are required if surprise could be orchestrated. The Soviets,
> in their modernizing, are reorganizing their forces for a fluid, granular form

---

[16]Richard Betts, *Surprise Attack: Lessons for Defense Planning* (Washington, D.C.: The Brookings Institution, 1982), p. 18.

of a non-linear, non-concentrated warfare that is entirely consistent with a preemptive surprise attack. In the revised Soviet approach, Group Soviet Forces, Germany has become the cutting edge of a Soviet attack.[17]

In such a situation, as Canby notes, the present family of CBMs lacks military relevance. They may even be militarily counterproductive, though NATO may still desire them for political reasons. Existing CBMs lack relevance because Soviet forces in being are already sufficiently large and of such a character that they do not need to move into exercise areas to launch a surprise attack. In fact, nowadays the very attempt to do so is a warning indicator in itself. Soviet forces can mobilize within their barracks, and most barracks in the German Democratic Republic are no more than 120 miles from the inter-German border. The dynamics of a surprise attack are such that the main forces do not need to hit the border initially. That is the task of heliborne ("desant") groupings, reconnaissance, special-armor raiding groups, and tactical airpower. The present family of CBMs was not designed to cope with the dynamics of force, or more specifically, the nature of its unfolding. Political scientists and foreign offices are unfamiliar with it; the military are protective and normally unwilling to consider any measure that could reduce their own flexibility, regardless of its effect upon opposing forces and overall political-military objectives.[18]

The authors of another important study concur with Canby's analysis and stress the difficult position NATO finds itself in as a consequence. "First," they note, "the decision to alert and mobilize NATO forces is inherently one to be made by NATO's political authorities. It is doubtful that any intelligence capability will be able to provide timely unambiguous warning....Hence, political leaders must be prepared to act on ambiguous warning, in order to provide time both for alerting and deploying forces, and, most important, for the preparation of forward defenses."[19] Pressures to avoid mobilization would be overwhelming. Before the fact, evidence of surprise attack cannot by definition be incontrovertible. NATO politicians

---

[17]"Arms Control, Confidence-Building Measures and Verification," in Edward C. Luck (ed.), *Arms Control: The Multilateral Alternative* (New York: NYU Press, 1983), pp. 200-201.

[18]*Ibid.*

[19]Report of the European Security Study (ESECS), *Strengthening Conventional Deterrence in Europe. Proposals for the 1980s* (New York: St. Martin's Press, 1983), p. 145.

may thus postpone those "dramatic (but time-sensitive) steps of mobilization and defense preparation which could in their view inadvertently escalate tension, thus endangering political crisis management, not to mention being highly disruptive and costly for the economy and civil life in general....Even more effective technical means and methods for intelligence collection, assessment and dissemination, cannot solve this dilemma," argues K. Peter Stratmann.[20]

CSBMs would not significantly increase strategic warning because the quality of U.S. intelligence sensors to monitor changes in postures, readiness and capabilities is already very high. The amount of intelligence evidence CSBMs—inspectors, for instance—could provide in a crisis situation over and above that yielded by technical and electronic sensors probably would be very limited. It might be difficult to distinguish preparations for a surprise attack from military activities aimed primarily at exercising military power for political purposes. Western political leaders taking decisions involving mobilization and alert measures most probably will have to act on ambiguous warning. CSBMs cannot change that fact.

It is perfectly possible to design a CSBM regime that would serve as an obstacle which a country planning a surprise attack would have to take into serious consideration. Unscheduled inspections are an example of this. So is the removal of equipment of a particularly offensive character such as bridging equipment, helicopters, artillery, assault vehicles, tanks and fuel pipelines. Limiting the scale of maneuvers and military movements might be another option. The extension of notification time might be relevant to a surprise-attack situation, even though loopholes would exist in a CSBM regime in the form of unannounced alerts. More ambitious plans might involve the setting up of special disengagement and buffer zones, where restrictions would be placed on such forces as mechanized units stationed inside the zones, as well as on tactical aircraft and helicopters. Such zones might raise the threshhold for military aggression and enhance political warning.

On the other hand, there are also counterarguments to such approaches. How does one differentiate between offensive and defensive military equipment? Are tanks and bridging equipment offensive instruments of war, or can they also be used in a defensive mode? Diplomatic and political

---

[20]*Ibid.*, p. 174.

obstacles to disengagement and buffer zones exist, both in the West and in the East. Earlier diplomatic experience in Europe regarding the negotiation of zones has not been very encouraging. The political reality of NATO's forward defense is not easily reconcilable with the concept of zones of disengagement. Nor is it necessarily obvious that such zones would favor the defensive side. Jonathan Alford notes that it is very hard to reconcile requirements for greater readiness with measures intended to make it more difficult for states to go to war. Measures to increase readiness, he points out, are moving in exactly the opposite direction from CBMs, and are almost irreconcilable with them, "for readiness to defend is almost indistinguishable from readiness to attack."[21] In short, many ideal proposals exist for disengagement-CSBMs, but not many of them are practical for the simple reason that no government is willing to damage its defense posture. General military thinking both in the East and in the West does not seem to favor military CBMs that curtail options, diminish flexibility and complicate force planning.

Restructuring force postures through negotiated CSBMs, therefore, does not seem to be feasible in the immediate future. Any such restructuring will apparently have to accompany a comprehensive political breakthrough between East and West in Europe. Accordingly, it does not seem possible to negotiate CSBMs which could effectively reduce what the NATO countries see as the most serious threat to European stability, i.e., the offensive military doctrine of the Warsaw Pact forces and their forward force posture and configuration. The alternative would seem to be to counteract surprise attack planning and execution through necessary changes in force postures, defense efforts and, if necessary, shifting the emphasis in NATO strategies in order to reduce vulnerability to such situations.

3. CSBMs and Crisis Prevention

If one looks at confidence- and security-building measures as "management instruments designed to reduce the pressures of arms on the process of politics during peacetime and on decision-making in crisis and war" (Holst), the necessity for creating adequate crisis-management

---

[21]Johnathan Alford, "Confidence-Building Measures in Europe: The Military Aspects," in *The Future of Arms Control, Part III: Confidence-Building Measures,* Adelphi Paper no. 149 (IISS).

mechanisms seems to be obvious. Such a mechanism should be tightly related to the implementation of an agreed CSBM regime in order to avoid unwanted interference by one alliance in the affairs of the other (the *driot de regard* problem). Crisis-management efforts should concentrate on clarifying the significance of military events and on elaborating measures which reduce ambiguity and defuse crises. One should, however, avoid the danger of over-institutionalization, as this could contribute to increased confusion and reduced flexibility. A simple mechanism would be preferable. Such a procedure would also have a constraining effect upon any country which might want to stage a crisis in order to activate a comprehensive crisis-management mechanism for political purposes.

4. The CDE Second Stage

The Madrid mandate envisages a review of the progress achieved in Stockholm to take place in the CSCE follow-up meeting in Vienna, scheduled for November 1986, and consideration of "ways and appropriate means for the participating States to continue their efforts for security and disarmament in Europe, including the question of supplementing the present mandate for the next stage of the conference...."

The original French proposal for the CDE, it will be recalled, envisaged a two-phased approach. The first phase — the CBM phase — would prepare for a second phase devoted to the reduction of armaments. Measures of information, observation, and notification would prepare the ground for more ambitious measures of reduction and verification in the second stage. Logically, it is difficult to dispute the link between confidence and disarmament. The more confident one feels about oneself and one's potential adversary the less the need for military strength. But it is by no means certain that it will be possible to negotiate a CSBM regime that will be conducive to a process of genuine arms control and disarmament. During the heyday of detente, for example, which was marked by a high degree of confidence among states, disarmament did not take place. In some cases the detente process actually resulted in increased levels of armaments.

The Madrid mandate, however, only charts the formal aspects of the future of the CDE. A number of issues remain to be clarified. First, a number of governments have yet to commit themselves to the second stage. Second, before one sees the final result of the first stage of the CDE, and, furthermore, before the Stockholm CSBMs are given a "trial run", a detailed discussion of a potential agenda for a CDE second stage would at this point be largely speculative.

From a formal viewpoint it is the Vienna CSCE follow-up meeting in November 1986 which will have to assess the work done in Stockholm and decide upon the modalities of the future of the CDE process. Theoretically, a number of options exist. In the current stage of East-West relations, though, it is difficult to imagine that the Vienna meeting will be able to negotiate a new mandate for the second, disarmament stage of the CDE. Rather, it can be expected that all proposals before the Stockholm Conference which the Conference does not have adequate time to consider or dispose of will eventually surface at the second stage of the CDE. It is of course also possible that the Vienna meeting may convene an expert meeting to assess implementation of first-stage CSBMs.

It should also be borne in mind that the Stockholm Conference and the military aspects of security are only parts of the whole CSCE process, with its carefully constructed balances between military security, economic and environmental matters, as well as human rights and human contacts (baskets one, two and three). Following the rather limited results of other CSCE meetings, like the human rights meeting in Ottawa, the cultural forum in Budapest, and the Bern meeting on human contacts, there is a growing feeling in the West that the East is turning its back on the human dimensions of the CSCE process to concentrate on the military aspects of security. The Soviet Union has always stressed "military detente", and Mikhail Gorbachev's proposal in East Berlin in April 1986 to convene a pan-European security conference would discuss military security issues from the Atlantic to the Urals. The future orientation of the CDE is thus clearly linked to the other aspects of the CSCE process. According to very strongly held Western positions, there has to be a balanced implementation, with progress and results in all important areas.

If a decision on a CDE second stage is to be taken, one is indeed struck by the complexity involved in negotiating disarmament and "associated measures" in a geographic area extending from the Atlantic to the Urals. In terms of compliance and verification measures that is a highly complicated task. As has already been pointed out, the CSCE forum of 35 participating countries, based on the principle of consensus, is clearly not a forum for speedy decisions.

In the final analysis, however, the CSCE process is the only forum in which all the main groups involved in the European security context participate. The process is slow and laborious, particularly in the field of military security. Nevertheless, it does have a potential for cooperation in the military security field. Yet, as noted above, it also has a potential for competition, power politics and rivalry. Ultimately, the CSCE/CDE process is about political and military influence and the distribution of power inside the existing European security order.

Viewed in a long-term political context, the process of building increased confidence in Europe is a slow and continuous process. CBMs should perhaps be viewed primarily as political commitments which are an integral part of the CSCE process, a cooperative undertaking in the military field that might have political implications. As such, they are ideally not only instruments for managing East-West military competition but are also potential instruments for better East-West relations. For that to happen, however, the "cooperative" elements in the CSCE process will have to prevail over the "competitive" ones.

5. The MBFR Connection

(a) *The Negotiations*

Efforts to achieve conventional disarmament or further military confidence-building within the CDE second stage (or a redefined mandate) would have a direct bearing on the ongoing MBFR negotiations. Practically and conceptually it is difficult to envisage the negotiation of conventional arms control being carried on in two different forums, even though the MBFR reduction area is much smaller than the CDE zone of application. Arguments have been put forward to integrate the two negotiating bodies, but one should also be aware that such integration would pose a number of practical and conceptual difficulties. The problems confronting the MBFR negotiators in Vienna will not disappear simply because of changing the negotiating modalities.

The arguments against the MBFR negotiating concept are well known. A basic theory in all arms control talks is that it is very difficult to obtain results in such talks unless the *demandeur* clearly shows that he is willing to obtain the same objectives unilaterally. Thus the Soviet Union is seen to have few motives to negotiate away its conventional superiority in the reductions area. It has also been pointed out that the reductions area is too limited in scope to be truly significant militarily. The geographical asymmetry is not favorable to NATO, as the Soviet forces to be withdrawn would be expected to fall back to positions some hundreds of kilometers away, whereas U.S. troops would have to be withdrawn across the Atlantic.

The ongoing NATO debate on new defense concepts and technologies will probably make the MBFR negotiations even more difficult.

On the other hand, the very fact that both parties have found it worthwhile to keep these negotiations going since 1973 clearly shows that they attach considerable value to these talks. The Soviet Union presumably has an interest in gaining insight into and possible leverage on Western defense planning through the MBFR talks, as an instrument for counteracting trends and developments not in its interest. Traditionally, the Soviet Union has had a special interest in establishing certain limits and restrictions on the Bundeswehr. Correspondingly, the MBFR talks also provide Western participants with insight into Warsaw Pact military thinking.

Following the initiation of the MBFR talks in 1973 a number of proposals and counterproposals have been launched. The mandate of the MBFR talks was defined in the Final Communique of June 28, 1973, in which the parties agreed to consider mutual reductions of forces and armaments and associated measures in central Europe. The general objective of these negotiations would be to contribute to a more stable relationship and to the strengthening of peace and security in Europe. Soviet objectives in the MBFR talks traditionally have been seen as attempts to:

- legitimize and formalize their numerical superiority in central Europe;
- obtain a *droit de regard* over the Bundeswehr; and
- inhibit NATO's force modernization programs.

Nevertheless, agreements in principle were gradually reached in Vienna on a number of important points, such as:

- reduction towards a common ceiling of 700,000 men for ground troops within a combined ceiling of 900,000 men for ground troops and air force personnel;
- a first-stage reduction involving only U.S. and Soviet troops with a consequent ceiling on U.S. and Soviet forces and a freeze on remaining force levels of other personnel; and
- associated measures (or confidence-building measures), such as notification of out-of-garrison activities, observation of such activities, notification of major military movements into the area, inspections within the reduction area, permanent exit/entry points, information exchanges on forces to be withdrawn and on the forces which are to remain.

As regards associated measures, however, the East has envisaged less effective measures. They thus rejected the extension of the area of confidence-building measures, inspections, permanent entry/exit points, and detailed information exchanges. They also rejected measures to verify limitations after reductions. Disagreements on the so-called data question, as well as on the associated measures, have long impeded progress in the MBFR talks. It has gradually become clear that negotiating a *comprehensive* MBFR agreement would be very complicated and perhaps impossible.

In February 1985, however, the East tabled a text for a first-phase agreement containing proposals for a limited U.S.-USSR troop reduction and a subsequent non-increase commitment on the part of all participants. In order to meet the Eastern first-phase proposal, the West in December 1985 announced a new move in which it set aside its long-standing requirement for an agreement on data prior to treaty signature and adopted a first-phase framework of limited duration. In January 1986 the West also tabled a Framework Document, including a Table of Associated Measures. The Western approach required detailed exchange of information and the introduction of an inspection regime involving 30 inspections per year in order to verify compliance with the non-increase commitment. A detailed exchange of information was considered necessary in order to establish a common data base for conducting inspections.

Following an initially negative Eastern reaction to the Western initiative, Soviet and East European official and media commentary began to moderate in tone. In his January 15, 1986 speech, General Secretary Gorbachev referred to the "contours of an agreement" emerging in Vienna, and also expressed Soviet willingness to make its proposed exit/entry points permanent. For a while optimism prevailed in Vienna and for the first time the parties were negotiating on the basis of a common framework.

The Eastern proposal of February 20, 1986, however, did not in any substantive way meet Western requirements. The East rejected Western demands for a detailed exhange of information and only agreed to give information on major formations. Agreement to on-site inspections would depend on the consent of the country requested, which could veto any such proposals.* The East also rejected Western requirements that

---

*In the Soviet view, national-technical means of verification would suffice.

Associated Measures 1 and 2 (notification of out-of-garrison activities and observation) would also apply beyond the reductions area. In one important area the East moved backwards, as it was made clear that Soviet troops on rotation would not pass through the exit/entry points. This would make verification of the commitment not to increase force levels nearly impossible.

In MBFR, as in the CDE, it is difficult to envisage substantial progress until the East adopts a more forthcoming attitude on such important issues as exchanges of information and inspection/verification. Any arms control agreement between East and West cannot be based predominantly on declarations of good intentions, as history all too often shows that intentions can change very quickly. Agreements that lack effective measures of verification would tend to undermine rather than strengthen East-West relations. Such agreements will not induce confidence in participants that agreements will be implemented and complied with. Thus, a simple commitment not to increase WTO and NATO forces in central Europe would be impossible to verify, inasmuch as the annual rotation of some 400,000 troops would be excluded. Force levels are very hard to verify without detailed, disaggregated information. Nor will confidence prevail if the party who is suspected of non-compliance can veto any request for inspection.

The Soviets argued that the Western associated measures were over-inflated, and not consistent with the modest first-phase reductions. Arguments about espionage, targeting and negative ("destabilizing") effects on the social order of the East were also heard. The East did not accept Western arguments that the information and verification measures were necessary chiefly in relation to the period in which both sides would agree not to increase their forces. So far, detailed Soviet proposals concerning the Gorbachev April 1986 proposal in East Berlin about a pan-European security conference have not been introduced into the Vienna process.

At present, therefore, it is difficult to predict the prospects for an agreement in Vienna. A first-phase agreement would probably be more significant in political than in purely military items. This is all the more true in that the most recent MBFR proposals suggest a certain reorientation away from the original troop reduction concept to the idea of associated (i.e., military confidence-building) measures. It would have a beneficial political impact in contributing to a stabilization of the security situation in Europe, and could prepare the ground for further reductions. The Soviet Union probably sees clear advantages in a first-phase agreement. While it would have only limited military significance, it would legitimize the Soviet presence in Eastern Europe in treaty form. Soviet participation in the Consultative Committee to be established after signature of a treaty would also facilitate Soviet efforts to influence West European policies and defense planning. The price that the Soviet Union would have to pay would be to accept an inspection and information regime that would make Eastern society somewhat more open and transparent in military and security terms. For the time being the Soviets do not seem to be willing to pay that price.

(b) *Theoretical Modalities*

Theoretically, one can envisage several models for integrating or relating the CDE and MBFR negotiations. A modest step would be to transfer MBFR Associated Measures 1 and 2 (notification of out-of-garrison activities and exchange of military observers) from MBFR to Stockholm. These have a wider range of application than the MBFR reduction area, and might be more easily negotiable inside the CDE Stage II. A more ambitious model would be to have a first-stage U.S.-Soviet agreement in Vienna, and then integrate the two negotiating forums. Again, theoretically, one can envisage a first stage CDE agreement and a first-stage MBFR agreement in Vienna which would result in the establishment of two different military arms control and CBM regimes in Europe.

A first-stage CDE agreement in Stockholm and continued MBFR stalemate in Vienna might open up several negotiating possiblities. One would be to convert the MBFR negotiations to a forum for East-West military discussion on strategies and military concepts (a conventional-arms talk shop), while transferring the troop reduction functions to the CDE II. In order to retain the alliance-to-alliance format of the troop-reductions negotiations, it might be possible to envisage a "two circles" regime inside the CDE, with the "old" MBFR negotiations constituting the inner circle.

On the face of it, such a solution would have certain appealing aspects. It might contribute to easing the West German ambivalence about the MBFR talks, caused by their concern that an agreement in MBFR might create a "special zone" of limitations on the FRG and the Bundeswehr. Such a solution would also respond to the long-standing NATO concern that the MBFR reduction area is too small, enabling the eventual reintroduction of Soviet (but not U.S.) forces. This solution might also accommodate French reservations about the MBFR talks, and bring them back to the negotiating table concerning conventional disarmament in Europe.

Nevertheless, such a merger of MBFR and CDE would run up against formidable obstacles. Whatever kind of circles one envisages in the CDE, the fact remains that the CDE framework—a thirty-five-country forum based on consensus—is on the whole not very usable for negotiating concrete arms control measures for conventional disarmament. Again, the data problem and all the other issues unresolved in MBFR will not simply disappear because of a change in the technical negotiating modalities. New life could be breathed into the MBFR negotiations by adopting the CDE geographical zone of application and including French and Soviet territory up to the Urals, but again, this may not be very realistic. As referred to above, the Gorbachev April 1986 proposal in East Berlin seems to relate mainly to the second stage of the CDE, reflecting previous Soviet positions on a pan-European security conference. The Soviets seem to envisage initial talks between the two alliances to which other countries would later adhere. The Soviets have not, however, introduced their proposal in either Stockholm or Vienna.

It does not, then, seem probable that any manpower or armaments reductions will be negotiated in either the CDE or the MBFR in the foreseeable future. This should not, however, prevent the participants in either body from negotiating partial agreements, which might also contain certain constraint measures. Constraints on military activities and force configurations which can reduce those components particularly well suited for offensive uses and rapid escalation should be carefully examined.

It can be argued that MBFR is a more suitable forum for these kinds of tasks than the CDE because of its alliance-to-alliance approach. Even if the MBFR negotiations have not produced concrete results (which could scarcely be expected given existing asymmetries), the Vienna forum has proved its value. The talks are important, professional, and unique as alliance-to-alliance negotiations on sensitive, complicated security issues.

Furthermore, a negotiating infrastructure has been established, in which it would also be feasible to discuss and negotiate issues relating to armaments, constraint measures and nuclear battlefield systems. These arguments, combined with the rather unwieldy and "political" character of the CDE, constitute a strong case for retaining MBFR as a full-fledged negotiating forum. Nuclear issues have been on the negotiating agenda of MBFR before. The Option III proposal put forward by the Western side in 1975 envisaged the reduction of NATO nuclear systems in return for Soviet withdrawal of ground forces and armaments. Option III was withdrawn as a result of the 1979 NATO double-track decision (which also led to the withdrawal of 1,000 Western nuclear weapons), but if nuclear battlefield systems once more were to be put on the East-West negotiating agenda, they would belong in the MBFR context, and not in the CDE. MBFR would then become the forum to negotiate battlefield-nuclear systems, cuts in conventional manpower or armaments, and zones of special restriction.

Finally, two more functions of MBFR may be pointed out. A number of observers have suggested adding a further dimension to the Vienna talks so that it becomes a forum for serious discussion of East-West military topics. Such a security dialogue could encompass a broad range of topics, from explaining the background of defense concepts to new technologies, structural reorganizations, and special military events. A security dialogue could also be used for clarifying misunderstandings and misperceptions.

Such a security dialogue could in itself constitute a confidence-building measure. Correspondingly, many suggestions have been informally advanced to institutionalize a multilateral mechanism for crisis control among the Vienna participants. A corresponding proposal has been put forward in Stockholm. These approaches should be explored further. At the same time, it should be made clear that one is not deliberating a shift in the MBFR mandate, and that the dominant task remains force reductions in central Europe. In any event, the relationship of MBFR to the CDE second stage will have to be determined in the light of the success of the CDE first stage.

VI.

Conclusion

In sum, while the Madrid mandate is predominantly oriented towards the (land-based and conventional) European security situation, the Stockholm Conference has also served as a forum for the broader, global superpower rivalry. Specifically, the Soviet Union has tended to treat the Stockholm Conference more as another forum for handling its bilateral ties with the United States than as a framework for regulating the European security order. Since the Stockholm CSBMs will apply to activities on European territories, the CDE is an inappropriate forum for the Soviet Union to handle its bilateral relations with the U.S. in nuclear and other military matters extending beyond Europe. In short, one may say that the Conference operates on various levels: as an arms control forum; as a political forum for East-West military cooperation within the framework of the CSCE; as a forum for U.S.-Soviet global superpower rivalry and East-West competition for political and military influence in Europe; and as a forum for political propaganda and influence.

In the political field the NATO countries in general have emphasized that, since the Stockholm conference is an integral part of the whole CSCE process, the military component should not be isolated from other elements of the CSCE process. As part of detente, the Helsinki Final Act was also a recipe for peaceful change in Europe, and was perceived as such by many European states. As Holst put it: "Confidence-building measures should be viewed as elements in a process for peaceful change of the post-war political order in Europe towards a more open, equitable and cooperative order."[23] In fact, the NATO countries never perceived the Helsinki Final Act as an embryo for a new collective security order in Europe. The West European members of NATO were particularly mindful of the fact that, taking into consideration Soviet military power

---

[23]Johan Jorgen Holst, "A CBM Regime in Europe: Prospects and Options for the Future. 23 Interrelated Propositions," Contribution in the Final Panel of a conference on "Confidence-Building Measures in the 80s," organized by the York University Research Programme in Strategic Studies and the Institute for East-West Security Studies, Montreal, October 15-16, 1984.

in Europe, the NATO alliance and the countervailing American influence through NATO were their best guarantor of military security.

The position of the neutral and non-aligned countries in Stockholm is more nuanced than that of the NATO countries, taking into consideration the diversity of strategic and political interests of the N/NA countries. However, the general approach of the N/NA countries (as reflected in their proposals) accords with the general orientation of the NATO proposals.

In terms of continuity and consistency, the Soviet proposals advanced in Stockholm deserve to be given high marks. They are essentially the same proposals which the Soviet Union has advocated for the last thirty years, and Soviet objectives appear to have remained the same. The Soviet flagship proposal in Stockholm has been the non-use of force treaty, originally put forward as a proposal for a collective security system in Europe. In retrospect, one may doubt if the Soviets had at any time a realistic concept of a collective European security system. In recent years, however, the non-use of force proposal has become a standard Soviet proposal, in compliance with the traditional Soviet approach towards negotiating European security affairs, which is to establish international legal and, perhaps even more importantly, political norms of relations between states.

The main objectives of this proposal — which the USSR no longer insists be incorporated in treaty form — are the establishment of a European security environment which would be conducive to overall Soviet security interests by maintaining the status quo in Eastern Europe while at the same time providing the Soviet Union with a *droit de regard* in West European security affairs through appropriate treaty consultation mechanisms. Indeed, both Soviet argumentation and a study of the proposal's provisions since it first materialized clearly show that the Soviet Union attaches great importance to the consultation mechanisms, which, were they ever to be effected, would legalize the Soviet assertion of its right to have a voice in West European security affairs. Such a mechanism would also serve as a useful instrument in influencing Western public opinion, as Soviet statements to this effect suggest.

Increasingly, the Soviet proposal on the non-use of force — whether in treaty or non-treaty form — has come to serve as a flexible "umbrella" for other Soviet proposals in the area of security and disarmament policy. Depending on the particular political context, the proposal has been put forward as an instrument that would prevent surprise attack or as a confidence-building measure in its own right. The latest version of the proposal also serves Soviet policy interests as regards outer space activities. In recent years the Soviets have incorporated their proposal for a no-first-use pledge into the non-use of force proposal. Since the NATO Alliance adopted the "flexible response" defense doctrine in 1967, a very important objective for Soviet defense policy has been to neutralize the NATO first-use option. The Soviets have tried to do this by acquiring their own theater nuclear capabilities as well as through arms control proposals. Such a policy would enhance Soviet conventional capabilities as well as weaken U.S. defense commitments to Europe. Soviet proposals for nuclear weapons-free zones serve the same purpose.

In this way, the Soviet proposal for an agreement on non-use of force serves as a framework for efforts to tip the balance of power in Europe in its own favor. It may even be argued that the non-use of force principle per se is of secondary importance compared to the other provisions contained in the broader Soviet proposal. A study of these provisions— whose evident goal is to neutralize and delegitimize NATO's defensive strategy—does not lead one to the conclusion that such an agreement would "give effect and expression to the duty of states to refrain from the threat of use of force in their mutual relations," as required by the Madrid mandate. As regards concrete confidence- and security-building measures, the Soviets seem to have a clear interest in CSBMs that would put a relatively low ceiling on allied NATO military activities (maneuvers) and affect independent naval and air activities in an extended zone of application, though it is by no means clear how strong this interest is, given the Soviet desire to maintain as much freedom of action for itself as possible.

Without doubt there exists a potential for future military confidence-building in Europe. At the same time, as has been shown, the obstacles are rather numerous. The differences in approach and the conflicting concepts of military confidence-building, as witnessed both before and during the Stockholm Conference, will make future work very difficult and clearly put a limit on how far the parties can pursue cooperative military confidence-building in Europe. Neither in the East nor in the West does there seem to be any marked enthusiasm for pursuing confidence-building measures that would seriously constrain military activities and options (thinning-out zones, reduced-deployment zones, restrictions on particular types of military equipment).

There are both military and political reasons for this. As I have tried to show in this study, NATO and the Warsaw Pact have been developing their arms control proposals along two separate and parallel tracks which are essentially as far apart today as they were thirty years ago, with the East concentrating on political measures and the West on concrete military measures. Yet, as has been pointed out before, the CSCE process is characterized by small steps, and the problem of building increased confidence in Europe should be seen as a continuous process.

As I have also tried to point out, CSBMs are not a panacea. They cannot change existing force postures or the character of superpower politics. They will probably not change existing tensions or enhance prospects for substantial arms control results. But as a component in an overall framework of a security policy encompassing CSBMs, arms control measures, and traditional diplomacy, CSBMs have a definite function and an important role to play. Furthermore, the development of confidence- and security-building measures in the CDE should be seen in the context of the entire CSCE process. In the end, it will not be possible to isolate the military component from the other components— political, economic, cultural and humanitarian—of the existing framework of security and cooperation in Europe. Clearly, arms control alone cannot bear the burden of East-West cooperation.

DEVELOPING A CONFIDENCE-BUILDING SYSTEM IN EAST-WEST RELATIONS: EUROPE AND THE CSCE

Adam-Daniel Rotfeld

Contents

I.

Introduction

The recent upsurge of interest by policy analysts and officials in confidence-building measures (CBMs) is reflected in the growing number of publications analyzing different aspects of the confidence-building process in Europe.[1] In general the analyses concentrate on the direct military effects and implications of certain specific types of measures. This military-technical oriented approach has tended to dominate the field.

The simple meaning of "confidence", however, is "the state of one that confides..., of feeling sure." Dictionaries indicate as synonyms of confidence the words trust, reliance, belief. The fundamental question, then, is: What are the existing causes of distrust and suspicion? Is it only a lack of clear and timely information about the nature of military activities of the countries on both sides of the East-West divide in Europe? After all, much of the sense of distrust prevalent in East and West would appear to be well founded, rooted as it is in profound clashes of national interests. How far is the risk of war between East and West actually connected with misunderstanding, miscalculation, or misperception? In other words, would Europe and East-West relations after the adoption of a set of purely militarily oriented CBMs be better off? What kind of role might these measures play in eliminating the causes of tension

---

[1]This study represents a continuation of my previous work on CSBMs. Fuller treatment of some points discussed here can be found in: "CBMs between Helsinki and Madrid: Theory and Experience," in F. Stephen Larrabee and Dietrich Stobbe (eds.), *Confidence-Building Measures in Europe* (New York: Institute for East-West Security Studies, 1983); the paper prepared for the Pugwash Workshop "CBMs in and for Europe," in W. Graf von Baudissin (ed.), *From Distrust to Confidence. Concepts, Experiences and Dimensions of CBMs* (Baden-Baden, 1983); the paper prepared for the seminar in Laxenburg, Austria (September 1982) published in Karl E. Birnbaum (ed.), *Confidence-Building and East-West Relations* (Laxenburg Papers, No. 3, March 1983); the article on "Military Constraints" (based on a presentation at a SIPRI colloquium, June 1984), *Polish Perspectives*, No. 3, 1984.

and dispelling distrust between East and West? Can CBMs in the military field be considered as the central and most important instrument in the confidence-building process, or should they be seen as an additional means, associated with the effort taken in many other fields, especially in the political, economic, cultural, and humanitarian areas, to reduce tension and promote cooperation in Europe?

It is the central thesis of this paper that, while military-oriented CBMs have a role to play in alleviating tensions and promoting confidence, they are inherently unable, by themselves, to address the underlying causes of suspicion and mistrust, i.e., the deeply rooted contest of specific national and alliance interests. Together with a series of broader diplomatic, arms control, and disarmament measures, military CBMs can perform a useful and stabilizing function. But it is critical not to put the cart before the horse. It is important, in short, that the problem of building confidence into East-West relations be put in proper perspective, that it be neither exaggerated nor denigrated.

Toward that end, this analysis will deal with the different perspectives in East and West on confidence-building in Europe, examining in particular the Conference on Security and Cooperation in Europe (CSCE) as an instrument of confidence-building in East-West relations. Within that context, I will analyze the role that confidence-building measures have played in the CSCE. What are the interrelationships, both between CBMs and the CSCE, and among the various kinds of CBMs? What are the possibilities, as well as inherent limitations, of CBMs in contributing to security and cooperation in Europe? It is important to remember that a substantial pre-history to the discussion exists, going back in some cases to the 1950s and even to the League of Nations, which in 1931 considered the idea of "moral disarmament" as an aspect of confidence-building in Europe. The study thus briefly looks at the heritage of such seminal events as the "Open Skies" proposal of 1955, the Geneva Surprise Attack Conference of 1958, as well as the elaboration of nuclear-free and other kinds of security zones. The core of the paper deals with the Stockholm Conference on Confidence- and Security-Building Measures (CSBMs) and Disarmament in Europe, and its potential to give an impulse to the creation of a genuine confidence-building system in Europe. The study concludes with some reflections on the relationship between such CSBMs and European security.

1. Different Dimensions of Confidence-Building in Europe

The latter half of the 1970s was marked by an increase in tension and hostility between East and West, particularly between the two superpowers. There were a variety of causes for this deterioration of East-West relations. Some were short-term and transient in character. Others are of a more permanent nature, and were determined by divergences in both national interests and the interests of the North Atlantic and Warsaw Treaty organizations. It would be an illusion, therefore, to attribute the deterioration of East-West relations mainly to factors of a subjective and temporary character. On the other hand, poor communication — related in particular to leadership changes in many countries — has had a detrimental effect on East-West relations.

Eastern and Western images and perceptions of each other's political objectives are a basic, though not decisive, element in determining each side's political goals. Indeed, images, especially in security policy, must be considered an important element of political reality. The concept of security embraces in equal measure the absence both of an actual threat and of the perception of threat. Very often national security policy is the product of imagined as well as real dangers. What really counts, it has been argued, is "what the actors involved think to be real."[2] Situations defined by men to be real tend to become real as a consequence of the interplay of perception and misperception. In Robert Jervis' view, "A decision-maker's image of another actor can be defined as those of his beliefs about the other that affect his predictions of how the other will behave under various circumstances."[3] The consequences of this inclination toward self-fulfilling prophecy can be quite far-reaching.

Psychological research suggests that, under conditions of high ambiguity produced by different signals and indicators from outside, statesmen, and thus states, have a tendency to turn inward, "relying less on the other's behavior and more on their preconceived image of the other."[4] It would be naive and unrealistic, however, to expect that channels

---

[2]Daniel Frei and Dieter Ruloff, *East-West Relations. Vol. 1: A Systematic Survey* (Cambridge, MA: Oelgeschlager, 1983), p. 3.

[3]Robert Jervis, *The Logic of Images in International Relations* (Princeton: Princeton University Press, 1970), p. 5.

[4]Floyd Allport, *Theories of Perception and the Concept of Structure* (New York: Wiley, 1955), p. 382, and Jervis, *op. cit.*, p. 225.

of communications (e.g., the "Hot Line" or permanent consultative bodies) or even a set of measures designed "to create greater openness and more predictability in military activities" can build or restore confidence between East and West and contribute effectively to reduce the risk of war.[5]

The main sources of tensions, threats to peace, and causes of wars are deeply rooted antagonisms and conflicts of interests. It is quite impossible to elaborate a workable, cooperative security system for East and West that is reduced exclusively or even primarily to the military sphere. In order to prevent an outbreak of war or at least to reduce its risk, it is not enough to deal with the military aspects of security (though they should not be underestimated), but rather to take into account all the factors and circumstances from which war might arise. The multilateral process initiated ten years ago in Helsinki was the most comprehensive and ambitious attempt to harmonize the conflicting interests of states from East and West and to replace confrontational and hostile postures with cooperative ones.

2. The CSCE Process as an Instrument of Confidence-Building in East-West Relations

The 35 member states of the Conference on Security and Cooperation in Europe (CSCE) agreed in Helsinki on a common goal: "...to give full effect to the results of the Conference and to assure, among their States and throughout Europe, the benefits deriving from those results and thus to broaden, deepen and make continuing and lasting the process of detente."[6] The significance of the adopted decisions consisted in setting into motion a multilateral process of cooperation in all spheres of international life. Among the elements, two should be mentioned as instrumental in initiating a confidence-building system in Europe:

  • the introduction of a common standard of behavior in international relationships ("code of conduct");

---

[5]"The Proposal of the Group of NATO Delegations in Stockholm," *Conference on Security and Cooperation in Europe/ Stockholm Conference. 1,* January 24, 1984, hereafter referred to as CSCE/SC (in Appendix).

[6]For the full text of the Helsinki Final Act see Edmund Jan Osmanczyck (ed.), *Encyclopedia of the United Nations and International Agreements* (Philadelphia: Taylor and Francis, 1985), pp. 333-334. The cited passage can be found on p. 333.

• the comprehensive character of the principles and other provisions adopted by the CSCE, which encompass practically all areas of their mutual relations (politics and the economy, inviolability of frontiers and human rights, military and humanitarian affairs, cooperation in the fields of culture and science, in education and the environment, in technology, transportation, tourism, in human contacts, in sport, information, etc.).

What is important in the CSCE process is that the participating states have given priority to their common interests over the differences which divide them. The CSCE provisions do not eliminate the sources of differences and controversies but instead create instruments to resolve conflicts through peaceful means, through negotiations, political consultation and cooperation.

In practice, all areas of international activities and mutual relations among the CSCE participating states should be adjusted to the set of rules adopted in Helsinki. The entire Final Act and the CSCE principles in particular constitute an integral whole.[7] These and other provisions were intentionally included in the Final Act in order to prevent a selective approach to the adopted decisions and to rule out any attempt at overemphasizing some principles at the expense of others. Officially, all countries reaffirmed in various ways the fact that, in accordance with the Final Act, each area is of equal importance to security and cooperation in Europe. In practice some NATO states, and in particular the United States, consider the human rights provisions as the centerpiece and the core of the whole CSCE process.[8] Such a reduction of the practical significance of the Helsinki Final Act to certain aspects of human rights (individual vs. collective, political vs. economic) was persistently pursued throughout

---

[7]The final clause of the "Declaration on Principles Guiding Relations between CSCE States" provides that "All the principles set forth above are of primary significance and, accordingly, they will be equally and unreservedly applied, each of them being interpreted taking into account the others." *Ibid.*, p. 334.

[8]One can find in some American writings the following interpretation of the CSCE Final Act: "For the first time in history, human rights were formally recognized in an international agreement as a fundamental principle regulating relations between states." William Korey, *Human Rights and the Helsinki Accord. Focus on U.S. Policy* (New York: Foreign Policy Association, Headline Series No. 264, 1983), pp. 15-17. Such comments ignore the UN Charter (art. 1, p. 3) and other documents, such as the Declaration of Human Rights or the Covenants on Human Rights.

all the stages of the CSCE to the detriment of other provisions, and especially of those regulating the areas of security and economic cooperation. Although the aim of the Helsinki Conference was to elaborate the framework of *inter-state relations,* the NATO countries focused mainly on the activities of individuals and non-governmental organizations in determining whether governments were complying with responsibilities — above all in the field of "human rights" — mandated by the Final Act. This approach reflected the specific political philosophy and ideological values of the Western countries.

The documents adopted in Helsinki, Belgrade and Madrid express a compromise between East and West. It would, however, be an over-simplification to say, as many American authors do, that "Basket One", "Questions Relating to Security in Europe," reflected principally the interests of the socialist countries, whereas "Basket Three", "Cooperation in Humanitarian and other Fields," suited the needs and the expectations of the NATO states.[9] One should not imagine the compromise as a simple trade-off, a "price" that had to be paid by WTO or NATO countries for adopting certain provisions virtually unacceptable to each. The compromise is expressed in an agreement reflecting a balance of interests not only in the document as a whole, but also in its parts and even in specific, carefully and thoroughly negotiated phrases and wordings of some provisions.

The CSCE process was "motivated by the political will, in the interest of peoples, to improve and intensify their relations and to contribute in Europe to peace, security, justice and co-operation as well as to rapprochement among themselves and with the other States of the world."[10] In other words, it was intended to establish a confidence-building system encompassing all areas of international activity. The central problem in achieving this goal was to find a balance between ends and means, which implies respect for socio-political diversity. On this basis it proved possible to codify principles and norms designed to constitute a joint regime for the territory of all European and North American states. Specific solutions were to be subordinated to these goals.

---

[9]See S.J. Flanagan, "The CSCE and the Development of Detente," in Derek Leebaert (ed.), *European Security: Prospects for the 1980s* (Lexington, MA: Heath, 1979), p. 190; Korey *op. cit.*

[10]*Encyclopedia of the United Nations and International Agreements, op. cit.,* p. 333.

The elements which proved to be the most essential in the confidence-building system in East-West relations established by the CSCE decisions can be characterized as follows:

- *multilateralism,* i.e., that all European states as well as the United States and Canada participate in the process initiated at Helsinki;
- the *democratic* nature of relations, i.e., that all 35 states take part in the CSCE process as sovereign, independent states and in conditions of full equality (all decisions being adopted by consensus);
- a *non-bloc approach,* according to which the Conference itself as well as the follow-up meetings to the CSCE are to be held "outside military alliances";[11]
- the *mechanism of continuity* of the initiated process, without creating a new organization;
- the *political nature* of obligations, whose effectiveness is based on the principle of commonality of interest, reciprocity and interdependence rather than on their mandatory character and legal validity;
- the *dynamic nature* of the CSCE process, i.e., that agreements and decisions do not set limits, but should be considered as a common foundation for the development of a new stage of East-West relations.[12]

All these elements are fully applicable to the mandate of the Stockholm Conference, adopted at the Madrid CSCE follow-up meeting.

3. CSBMs and the CSCE: Interrelationships, Limitations, Possibilities

The problem of participation, procedure, working methods and other modalities adopted for the CSCE apply also to the Stockholm Conference. This was agreed to as part of the Madrid mandate and was not subject

---

[11]"Final Recommendations of the Helsinki Consultations," para. 65, in Adam-Daniel Rotfeld (ed.), *From Helsinki to Madrid. CSCE Documents* (Warsaw, 1983), p. 103.

[12]"Today it is the maximum of the possible, but tomorrow it should become the starting point for making further headway along the lines mapped out by the Conference." Concluding Statement on the III Stage of the CSCE made by the Head of the Soviet Delegation, Helsinki, July 30-August 1, 1975. *CSCE. Verbatim Records and Documents. CSCE-III,* PV. 3, p. 65.

to controversy.[13] Problems related to the character of the linkages between the CSCE and the Stockholm Conference were, however, debated. Beforehand it was not clear how far the multilateral process of confidence-building in the military field should be considered an integral part of the CSCE nor, consequently, what kind of link would be most appropriate between the Stockholm Conference and the follow-up meetings to the CSCE.

In the early 1970s, before the Helsinki Conference, the Warsaw Treaty countries argued that the military aspects of European security should be discussed in a separate forum. In Vienna the talks on Mutual Reductions of Forces and Armaments in Central Europe (MFR) were initiated as the result of Soviet-American negotiations. Originally, the Warsaw Treaty countries proposed to invite all European states to Vienna, members of the alliances as well as neutral and non-aligned countries. NATO preferred to conduct the talks within an alliance framework. It was finally agreed to start the Vienna talks on January 31, 1973, with a group of 11 countries having the status of direct participants and a special status for 8 additional participants.[14] Simultaneously, in the framework of the preparatory negotiations which were held in Helsinki (November 23, 1972 - June 8, 1973), it was decided to include confidence-building measures in the agenda of the CSCE (para. 22-24 of the Final Recommendations of the Helsinki Consultations). Particular interest in the military dimension of the CSCE was shown early on by the group of non-bloc countries, by Romania and by some of the smaller NATO states, such as Norway, Denmark, and the Netherlands. The reluctance of the global powers to embrace the idea of CBMs was influenced by different considerations. The Soviet Union

---

[13]See *Decisions of the Helsinki Preparatory Meeting on the Agenda, Time-table and other Organizational Modalities for the First Stage of the Conference on Confidence-and Security-Building Measures and Disarmament in Europe* (Helsinki, 1983), p. 5.

[14]Those in the category with direct participant status of the WTO and NATO whose territories fall within the area of potential reductions (GDR, Poland and Czechoslovakia on one side and the FRG, Belgium, Netherlands and Luxembourg on the other) and states whose armed forces are stationed in this zone (the U.S., Great Britain, and Canada on the NATO side and the USSR on the WTO side). Those having a special status are, from the WTO, Bulgaria, Hungary and Romania; and from NATO, Denmark, Norway, Greece and Turkey. See W. Multan (ed.), *Vienna Talks on Mutual Reduction of Forces and Armaments in Central Europe. Selection of Documents 1973-1978* (texts in English and Polish) (Warsaw, 1980).

initially considered Western insistence on CBMs as an attempt to introduce an imbalance in East-West relations in general and in Soviet-American relations in particular, for the territories of the United States and Canada were completely exempt from the application of the proposed measures. In addition, the whole concept of CBMs was seen as an element of the Western philosophy of arms control, emphasizing monitoring and verification instead of disarmament and arms reduction. On the other hand, the lack of U.S. interest in elaborating CBMs within the framework of the CSCE process was connected most probably with the U.S. concern about the effectiveness of such measures on a multilateral basis. Futhermore, both the Soviet Union and the United States applied certain measures in their bilateral relations which were sufficient to verify their compliance with agreements they had concluded. This encompassed agreements made just after World War II in the framework of the Allied Control Commission for Germany, as well as those concluded in the 1960s and 1970s for monitoring the limited nuclear test-ban treaty, establishing the telecommunications link between Moscow and Washington ("Hotline"), observing the SALT I accord through national-technical means (satellites), and the operation of the Standing Consultative Commission. Nevertheless, as a result of the negotiations during the second stage of the CSCE in Geneva (1973-1975), the "Document on Confidence-Building Measures and Certain Aspects of Security and Disarmament" was adopted as an integral part of the Helsinki Final Act and in precise accordance with the mandate.[15]

The main goal of the N/NA countries was to reflect in the CSCE final document, as the Yugoslav representative put it, "the entire range of security measures in the military field, from confidence-building measures to general and complete disarmament."[16] This kind of expectation spoke volumes for the overly ambitious and unrealistic hopes of some neutral and non-aligned participants, who aimed to break the monopoly of the

---

[15]See text in Appendix. Prior notification of major military manuevers is considered by Ljubivoje Acimovic, head of the Yugoslav CSCE Delegation, as "the only measure that the Final Recommendations from Helsinki (1973) had specifically charged the Conference with adopting." See Ljubivoje Acimovic, *Problems of Security and Cooperation in Europe* (Alphen aan den Rijn:Sijthoff & Noordhoff, 1981), p. 218. In fact, the mandate adopted in Helsinki mentioned also, in para. 23, "the exchange of observers by invitation at military manuevers under mutually acceptable conditions." It also suggested to study "the question of major military movements." Text in Rotfeld (ed.), *From Helsinki to Madrid, op. cit.,* p. 92.

[16]Acimovic, *op. cit.,* p.216.

global powers in the field of military security, arms control and disarmament. Needless to say, this was neither feasible nor necessary, and the effects were predictable. The document agreed to in Helsinki reflected the gap between the broad goals set for confidence-building measures and those concrete measures actually included in the Final Act. The very fact that this idea, despite all its ambiguity and the limited scope of the adopted measures, was at least recorded in the Final Act is most important in terms of the Helsinki process. On this basis, subsequent efforts might be undertaken to achieve its full realization.[17]

The aims of CBMs, as provided for in the Final Act, are as follows:

- to eliminate the causes of tensions;
- to strengthen confidence and to contribute to increased stability and security in Europe;
- to reinforce the principle of the non-use of force;
- to reduce the danger of armed conflicts and of misunderstanding or miscalculation of military activities, which could give rise to apprehension ("particularly in a situation where the participating States lack clear and timely information about the nature of such activities").[18]

The modest set of practical measures and the low degree of commitment to the CSCE provisions in the military sphere have often been the subject of legitimate criticism.[19] Many politicians and experts in the West (as well as in the East) would like to use CBMs as an instrument of fundamental change of the political and strategic order in Europe.[20] These hopes, even if limited only to the Stockholm Conference, are unlikely to be realized. While changes in the character of East-West relations are possible, they will be produced as the result of a long historical process, rather than as the outcome of this or that conference or summit meeting. The entire process initiated at Helsinki (including CBMs) cannot be seen simply as an element of the struggle between contending visions of the future.

---

[17]*Ibid.*, p. 229.

[18]*Encyclopedia of the United Nations and International Agreements, op. cit.*, p. 334.

[19]See Rotfeld (ed.), *op. cit.*, p. 97.

[20]James E. Goodby, "The Stockholm Conference: A Report on the First Year," *Department of State Bulletin*, February 1985, p. 5.

Negotiations, of course, include by definition elements of struggle and cooperation. Yet they also imply gradual progress from a Manichaean world view, where everything is seen in an oversimplified way ("the children of light vs. the children of darkness"), to a more realistic vision. After all, even devils are fallen angels.

Negotiations in general, and in the East-West context in particular, involve give-and-take. Therefore, the presentation of their outcome as a victory in battle is neither helpful nor convincing.[21] Documents adopted on the basis of consensus are not a simple compilation of each side's desires. They reflect a common political will and therefore cannot be presented as "our provisions which they felt obliged to accept." Under these conditions CBMs can play a positive role and introduce an innovative element only through promoting the idea of cooperative security between East and West. This means in practice that appropriate procedures and working methods of negotiation, proceeding from the CSCE provisions, be applied to developing such CBMs. The solution adopted in the Final Act in this respect envisaged organizing meetings among representatives of the 35 States with the aim of proceeding "through the exchange of views both on the implementation of the provisions of the Final Act and of the tasks defined by the Conference, as well as in the context of the question dealt with by the latter, on the deepening of their mutual relations, the improvement of security and development of co-operation in Europe, and the development of the process of detente in the future." For ten years now this passage has been subject to different interpretations.

The preparatory meetings in Belgrade and Madrid examined whether follow-up conferences should concentrate on the past or on the future. The NATO countries opted for the concept of a "Review Conference", with the right of monitoring and evaluating the implementation process, whereas the WTO States argued for meetings oriented toward the improvement of mutual relations. The compromise reached in Madrid reflected a delicate balance of interests. The most important element of this balance is the mandate for the Stockholm Conference, which reflects more than

---

[21]"Our job," according to Max Kampelman, the head of the American delegation to the CSCE Follow-up Meeting in Madrid, "is to tell the world that the Soviet authorities felt obliged to accept *our* provisions on human rights and the self-determination of peoples, and exploit these provisions to maximum effect in *our* public diplomacy." Max M. Kampelman in conversation with George Urban, "Can We Negotiate with the Russians? (And If So, How?)," *Encounter,* March 1985, p. 29.

a CSCE meeting of experts due to its political nature and continuous character. On the other hand, the interrelationship with the Vienna follow-up meeting is established by the following provision: "...a future CSCE follow-up meeting will consider ways and appropriate means for the participating States to continue their efforts for security and disarmament in Europe, including the question of supplementing the present mandate for the next stage of the Conference on Confidence- and Security-Building Measures and Disarmament in Europe."[22]

4. Evolution and Development

(a) Moral Disarmament

Although most analysts trace the gestation of the concept of confidence-building measures to the CSCE and the Helsinki Final Act, in fact the idea is much older. In 1931 the Polish government introduced into the League of Nations a "Memorandum Concerning the Attainment of Moral Disarmament."[23] The document declared that mutual confidence "in large measure depends on securing an improvement in the moral and political situation in Europe." The Polish proposal thus envisaged specific changes in criminal codes individualizing responsibility for aggression (thus anticipating Nuremburg), the condemnation of war as an instrument of foreign policy, and the prohibition of "propaganda aimed at disturbing friendly relations." National education systems were to be restructured in this spirit: instruction on the purposes of the League and revision of school texts were the order of the day.[24] Like all such efforts at collective security in the interwar period, the Polish initiative foundered on the rise of forces hostile to peace and, thus, to all efforts to shore up international confidence.

The search for multilateral confidence-building measures in Europe after World War II is associated with three different initiatives: "Open Skies," denuclearized and security zones, and the prevention of surprise attack.

---

[22]The mandate of the Stockholm Conference is a part of the Concluding Document of the Madrid CSCE Follow-up Meeting and is included as an Annex to *Decisions of the Helsinki Preparatory Meeting on the Agenda, Time-Table and other Organizational Modalities for the First Stage of the Conference on CSBMs and Disarmament in Europe* (Helsinki, 1983), p. 4 (see Appendix, *infra*).

[23]*League of Nations Document*, no. C. 602.M.240 (1931), IX, United Nations Archives.

[24]*Ibid.*

(b) *"Open Skies"*

The proposal presented by U.S. President Dwight D. Eisenhower at the Geneva summit conference (July 21, 1955) focused on the problem of mutual aerial inspection. The American initiative and the Soviet reaction reflected the fundamental divergence of approach of both global powers to the problem of confidence- and security-building. President Eisenhower, addressing his statement to the leaders of the Soviet Union, proposed:

- "To give to each other a complete blueprint of our military establishments, from one end of our countries to the other; lay out the establishments and provide the blueprints to each other.

- "Next, to provide within our countries facilities for aerial photography to the other country...and by this step to convince the world that we are providing as between ourselves against the possibility of great surprise attack, thus lessening danger and relaxing tension."[25]

The American delegation in the UN Subcommittee on Disarmament was instructed to give "priority effort to the study of inspection and reporting." Such a system, Eisenhower stated, would do much to develop mutual confidence.

Eisenhower's proposal was rejected by the Soviet Union. The counter-arguments were as follows:

- "... aerophotography cannot give the expected results, because both countries stretch over vast territories in which, if desired, one can conceal anything.

- "... the proposed plan touches only the territories belonging to the two countries, leaving out the armed forces and military constructions situated in the territories of other states."[26]

Walt Rostow, an active participant in the preparation of Eisenhower's proposal, has made some revealing remarks about the background of the American initiative. At the time of the Geneva summit, according to Rostow, the United States was at work on a program to photograph the USSR, both from balloons and from U-2 aircraft, then under development. Possibilities of satellite photography were also under discussion.

---

[25]U.S. Department of State, *Documents on Disarmament 1945-1959,* vol. I, (1945-1957) (Washington, D.C.: U.S. Government Printing Office, 1960), pp. 487-488. For the text, see Appendix.

[26]*Ibid.,* doc. 125, p. 496.

According to Rostow, American policy-makers were aware of these possibilities. One can assume that, in Eisenhower's opinion, "the U.S. position would be stronger in the future with regard to unilateral aerial photography if the Open Skies offer were made before the U.S. flights over the USSR began."[27]

For a proper understanding of the motives of both global powers it is useful to recall the report of the Quantico Panel (June 10, 1955), organized by Assistant Secretary of State Nelson Rockfeller. Its main idea was that the United States enjoyed as of 1955 a significant military advantage over the Soviet Union. The American proposals in Geneva (including mutual aerial inspection) should test Soviet willingness to make concessions and to improve the U.S. position. According to Rostow, "That was the Quantico Panel's doctrine."[28] These aims were far from the official arguments highlighted in the president's statement. Given the admitted military imbalance in favor of the U.S., and the comparative intelligence advantage that would have accrued to the U.S. if the Open Skies plan had been adopted, Soviet resistance to this "confidence-building" proposal is readily understandable. One lesson for the future was that for a measure actually to create confidence, instead of heightened mistrust and suspicion, it had to be rooted in a balance of interests — political and military — for any chance of adoption. The failure of "Open Skies" suggests that military parity and the relationship of proposed measures to a specific disarmament regime constitute two critical elements of success.

(c) *Atom-free and Security Zones*

Proposals first advanced in the 1950s for nuclear weapons-free zones represented an important step toward introducing elements of confidence, stability and restraint into East-West relations. The most fully developed plans for denuclearization were addressed to central Europe as the region characterized by the greatest peacetime concentration of troops and armaments, both conventional and nuclear, in history. In presenting the first version of the well known plan that bears his name, the Polish Minister of Foreign Affairs, Adam Rapacki, said (October 2, 1957):

---

[27]W.W. Rostow, *Open Skies. Eisenhower's Proposal of July 21, 1955* (Austin, Texas: University of Texas Press, 1982), p. 12.

[28]*Ibid.*, p. 12; see also pp. 26-33.

"... [W]e have felt that it would be useful to set up limited and controlled armaments zones in Europe.... In the interest of Poland's security and of a relaxation of tension in Europe, and after consultation with the other parties of the Warsaw Treaty, the Government of the People's Republic of Poland declares that if the two German States should consent to enforce the prohibition of the production and stockpiling of nuclear weapons in their respective territories, the People's Republic of Poland is prepared simultaneously to institute the same prohibition in its territory."[29]

On February 14, 1958, Rapacki presented the second version of the plan, which set out in detail the territorial scope (Poland, Czechoslovakia and the two German states) as well as the substantative obligations of this commitment.[30] The idea of a limited armaments zone, a neutral belt in the center of Europe or some other special arrangement in the region where the military forces of NATO and the WTO confront each other, recurred in a number of proposals presented by both Eastern and Western countries. The geographic scope of the proposed zones varied and was not always identical with the frontiers of the countries covered by the envisioned regime of disengagements.[31] Two problems preoccupied the authors of most of the disengagement proposals for central Europe: military security and political issues connected with the German question. All of these plans, including the four versions of the Rapacki Plan, were rejected by the NATO countries. The main objections were of a military and political character. The U.S. note in response to the Polish Government stated that the proposals

are too limited in scope to reduce the danger of war or provide a dependable basis for security in Europe. They neither deal with the essential question of the continued production of nuclear weapons by the present nuclear powers nor take into account the fact that present scientific techniques are not adequate to detect existing nuclear powers. The proposed plan does not affect the central sources of power capable of launching a nuclear attack,

---

[29]Text in U.S. Dept. of State, *Documents on Disarmament 1945-1959,* vol. II (1957-1959), *op. cit.,* doc. 225, pp. 890-892.

[30]*Ibid.,* doc. 244, p. 944.

[31]By way of illustration one can mention the initiatives presented by the leaders of the Labour Party (Dennis Healey and Hugh Gaitskell), by the British Prime Minister Anthony Eden, and by the French politicians Pierre Mendes-France and Jules Moch. The first proposal for a nuclear weapons-free zone in central Europe was made on March 27, 1956 by the USSR in a subcommittee of the UNDC. See Adam-Daniel Rotfeld, "In Search of a Security Zone in Europe," *Polish Perspectives,* no. 2, 1983, pp. 21-32.

and thus its effectiveness would be dependent on the good intentions of countries outside the area.[32]

For a variety of reasons, relating mainly to concerns about dividing the NATO alliance into separate security zones and a preference for a nuclear-based strategy, the U.S. and its NATO allies have resisted calls for the establishment of security zones in Europe. These objections, rooted in preoccupation with alliance management rather than with the broader issues of East-West security, have led to an impasse that must be considered a major lost opportunity in East-West relations, both in the military and political spheres.

(d) *Prevention of Surprise Attack*

In this question, as well as in the entire process of disarmament negotiations, the main reason for the deadlock was the priority given by NATO to international inspection and control, whereas for the WTO verification does not constitute a value as such, but rather is functionally related to substantive agreement on disarmament and arms limitations. Nevertheless, in 1958 a convergence of positions was detectable on the problem of preventing surprise attack. In preparing the mandate of a meeting of experts on this subject, the Soviet Union stressed the necessity of working out practical recommendations concerning measures to prevent surprise attack in combination with specific steps in the field of disarmament. The Soviet government expressed its readiness to reach an agreement on establishing a broad set of verification measures: control posts at railway centers, large ports, and major highways, in combination with specific disarmament measures; concerning aerial photography, the Soviet Union declared itself ready to accept this kind of inspection in areas of key military significance so as to minimize the danger and fear of surprise attack.[33] The difference between the two sets of papers presented at the Geneva Conference was characterized by the U.S. representative during the concluding session in the following words: "The contrast between these two sets of documents is self-evident. We have sought to promote *technical* discussion and understanding. You [i.e., the USSR] have sought discussion of a selection of *political* proposals, for the most

---

[32]U.S. Dept. of State, *Documents on Disarmament 1945-1959*, vol. II, *op. cit.*, pp. 1023-1025.
[33]*Ibid.*, doc. 282, p. 1085 and doc. 294, p. 1137.

part not susceptible of technical assessment."[34]

The Soviet Union took part in this conference under the assumption that the first steps toward preventing surprise attacks would be useful "if they included, in addition to a number of control and inspection measures, definite disarmament measures."[35] The Conference on the Prevention of Surprise Attack did not succeed. Nevertheless, the political significance of the Geneva experts meeting is still valid. It provided, for the first time, the opportunity in a multilateral East-West forum for a thorough exchange of views on the problem of preventing surprise attack. That the positions taken over 25 years ago remain fundamentally unchanged is not encouraging. During the concluding session the Soviet delegate expressed the view that, "The Western Powers are separating control [inspection] from practical measures for preventing a surprise attack and see in control nothing but the acquisition of information about the defensive readiness of the Socialist countries."[36] This sounds as up-to-date as would be a quotation taken from a Soviet speech at the Stockholm Conference in 1985 or 1986. It would seem that an examination of the Geneva experts meeting of 1958 can serve as a significant source not only for students and historians, but also for officials and analysts in search of new, effective confidence- and security-building measures in Europe. In fact, it appears that many of the solutions first proposed in Geneva a generation ago will not see the light of day for some time to come.[37]

---

[34]*Ibid.*, doc. 355, p. 1317.

[35]*Ibid.*, doc. 336, p. 1325

[36]*Ibid.*, p. 1332.

[37]My skepticism is rooted in the lack of interest in CSBMs among U.S. military specialists. Several authors are most pessimistic in their forecasts: "Like the Helsinki measures, the best that can probably be hoped for any compromise agreements emerging from Stockholm is not that they build confidence and security but simply that they lessen mutual feelings of distrust and insecurity (as, for example, crisis management measures might), while holding open the possibility of greater progress at some later date." Richard E. Darilek, "Building Confidence and Security in Europe. The Road to and from Stockholm," *The Washington Quarterly*, Winter 1985, p. 139.

5. After Helsinki, Before Madrid

The idea of holding special consultations between representatives of the CSCE countries on military aspects of security was put forward at the Belgrade Meeting by the Soviet delegation (October 24, 1977).[38] It suggested that military experts discuss the following questions: conclusion by the CSCE states of a treaty renouncing first-use of nuclear weapons; preparation of an agreement on non-expansion of the North Atlantic and Warsaw Treaty organizations (i.e., the non-admission of new members to either grouping);[39] and further development of the confidence-building measures envisaged in the Final Act (e.g., limiting maneuvers to a maximum of 50-60,000 troops) and their application to the entire Mediterranean region, given the favorable response of the countries of that area. The Soviet representatives in Belgrade argued that agreements on these questions would have diminished the possibility of an outbreak of war in Europe, checked the further hardening of bloc divisions in Europe (chiefly in connection with the prospective accession of Spain to NATO), and helped to reduce tensions, military confrontation and the war psychosis that increasingly accompanies large-scale exercises involving hundreds of thousands of troops in a zone stretching all the way from the far north of Norway to Turkey in the south.

The NATO countries rejected in its entirety the military detente package proposed by the Soviet Union. The Concluding Document of the Belgrade Meeting was largely a formal summary of the proceedings. Its substantive decisions boiled down to two elements: 1) the participants "reaffirmed the resolve of their Governments to implement fully, unilaterally, bilaterally and multilaterally, all the provisions of the Final Act";[40] 2) it was agreed to convene the next CSCE meeting in Madrid and to hold a number of meetings of experts, thus ensuring the continuity of the process initiated at Helsinki.

---

[38]The official title of the Soviet proposal was: "Programme of Action with a View to the Consolidation of Military Detente in Europe." CSCE/Belgrade Meeting (BM)/5.

[39]Proposals for a no-first-use treaty and non-expansion of existing military and political groupings were first put forward by the Warsaw Treaty states in the Declaration of the Political Consultative Committee adopted at Bucharest (November 25-28, 1976).

[40]Concluding Document of the Belgrade Meeting in Rotfeld (ed.), *From Helsinki to Madrid. CSCE Documents, op. cit.*, p. 214.

The question of a conference of CSCE representatives on military aspects of security, however, was left unresolved. On March 9, 1978, at the closing session, the French representative referred to his government's official statements concerning a European Disarmament Conference.[41] As he saw it, the aim of the Conference, to be attended by all the countries of Europe plus the United States and Canada, would be in the first place to examine the sources of instability and insecurity in Europe. As evidence of these he pointed to "the excessive stocks of conventional weapons in Europe and the possibility of surprise attack with all its ensuing consequences."[42] On May 24-25, 1978, the French Government circulated memoranda and information on the proposed European Disarmament Conference. The French plan envisaged two stages of negotiations: the first to be devoted to confidence-building measures and the second to the limitation of conventional weapons. The Conference decisions would apply to continental Europe according to the formula, "from the Atlantic to the Urals." The idea was to exclude the limitation of nuclear weapons and naval forces from the agenda, though both are crucial components of the national security of different countries, as well as of the military situation and stability in the whole of Europe. This approach obtained the support of France's allies in NATO.[43] The communique of the Ministerial Session in Brussels (December 14, 1979) announced that the NATO countries wanted the negotiations on confidence-building measures to take place "under the aegis of the CSCE" and to produce CBMs that were "militarily significant," "verifiable," "politically binding," and "applicable to the entire continent of Europe."

Parallel to the French initiative, the Warsaw Treaty states put forward in May 1979 a proposal for a Conference on Military Detente and Disarmament in Europe.[44] At the next meeting of the Warsaw Treaty Foreign

---

[41]CSCE/BM/V.R.3 For a French assessment of the Soviet proposal, see J.-Ch. Romer, "L'URSS et la Conference de Stockholm. Une question de confiance," *Defense Nationale,* August-September 1984, p. 45.

[42]*Ibid.*

[43]"Kommunique ueber die Ministertagung des Nordatlantikrats in Brussel (December 13-14, 1979)," *Europa Archiv. Dokumente. 1980* (Bonn: Deutsche Gesellschaft fuer Auswaertige Politik, 1980), pp. D38-D43.

[44]Communique of the Foreign Ministers Committee of the Warsaw Treaty States, Budapest, May 15, 1979, *Zbior Dokumentow PISM* (no. 4-6, 1979), p. 300.

Ministers Committee (Berlin, December 5-6, 1979), notes were compared on the results of contacts and consultations with representatives of other CSCE countries: it turned out that both the Warsaw Treaty and the NATO states were in favor of attendance by all the CSCE participants and of holding the conference in two stages. Consequently, what was debated at the Madrid Meeting of the CSCE was not so much *whether* there was a need to convene a special conference devoted to military confidence-building measures but rather *the aims and terms of reference* of such a meeting.

6. The Madrid Meeting

Both East and West believe that confidence and security are closely linked. Where they differ is over perceptions of the essence of security and, more importantly, the ability and will to respect each other's security interests. At Madrid, proposals were tabled by five states: Poland (December 8, 1980), France (December 9, 1980), Yugoslavia (December 12, 1980), Romania and Sweden (both December 15, 1980). The drafting of the conference mandate came to dominate the business of the Madrid CSCE meeting.

Given the consensus on adopting CSCE rules of procedure to the CBM conference, it was possible to identify certain elements common to both East and West. These items of accord included the following points:

a) the participants should be the 35 states involved in the process initiated at Helsinki;

b) attendance should, in accordance with the Helsinki Final Recommendations, take place on a basis of democracy and equal rights and "outside military alliances";

c) the negotiations should be held in stages, the first to be devoted to confidence-building measures.

Differences centered on both the general concept of the first stage and the specifications of its task, particularly the definition of the criteria which should be met by the Conference decisions. Here the Polish proposal, seconded by the other Warsaw Treaty states, left the participants a substantial margin of maneuver. By contrast the French position, backed by the NATO countries, rigidly postulated the development of a "coherent system of CBMs" applicable to the entire European continent from the Atlantic to the Urals. In other words, its basis was the supposition that threats to European security could only come from land-based military activity. Beyond that, the NATO countries wanted strict criteria to which any subsequent decisions had to correspond. Thus, the French proposal stipulated that all confidence-building measures should be militarily significant, politically binding, and verifiable. It also called for the division of these measures into three categories: *informational*, making for a better overview of armed forces; *stabilizational*, aimed chiefly at notification of military activity (prior notification according to specified parameters of the scope and size of military activity); and, lastly, *observational and monitoring*, for verification of the obligations undertaken.

The Yugoslav, Romanian, and Swedish proposals[45] also opted for a two-stage conference. In contrast to the NATO position, however, Yugoslavia, Romania, and Sweden stressed in their submissions that the aim of the first stage of the conference should be not so much to devise measures of an informational and observational nature as to limit military activity and prepare the ground for disarmament, both conventional and nuclear. As regards specific suggestions for the first stage of the Conference, the Swedish proposal tended to converge with the NATO position. It envisaged concentrating in this phase on confidence-building measures that furthered the openness of military activities. A similar line was taken at the beginning of the Madrid Meeting by many representatives of the NATO states. But the measures of restraint and disengagement proposed by the Swedes failed to win their sympathy. The Norwegian Foreign Minister, Knut Frydenlund, expressed the view that the confidence-building measures adopted in the Helsinki Final Act had more to do with the role than the level of armed forces in Europe and were designed to introduce elements of "predictability and transparency."[46]

It was agreed relatively quickly that there was a need to frame a broader concept of CBMs than the ones listed in the Final Act, since no one questioned that they were too modest in scope to make a significant contribution to reducing the military confrontation in Europe. It was decided that future measures would serve the purpose of advancing not only confidence, but also security. A new term was coined: Confidence- and Security-Building Measures (CSBMs). This was not merely a technical change, but expressed a broader political concept.

---

[45]CSCE/RM (Madrid Meeting). 27, CSCE/RM.31, and CSCE/RM.34, respectively.
[46]CSCE/RM/VR.4, p. 13.

II.

The Stockholm Conference:
Tasks, Expectations, Prospects

1. The Mandate of the Stockholm Conference

The mandate of the Stockholm Conference as specified in the Madrid Concluding Document is reflected in both the concrete provisions and the actual designation of the Conference which, officially, is the "Conference on Confidence- and Security-Building Measures and Disarmament in Europe." The essence of the mandate adopted in Madrid is reflected in the following paragraph:

> On the basis of equality of rights, balance and reciprocity, equal respect for the security interests of all CSCE participating States, and of their respective obligations concerning confidence- and security-building measures and disarmament in Europe, these confidence- and security-building measures will cover the whole of Europe as well as the adjoining sea area and air space. They will be of military significance and politically binding and will be provided with adequate forms of verification which correspond to their content.[47]

All the elements of this formula are subject to various interpretations. However, the chief source of controversy during the negotiation in Madrid, which was only partly resolved and had to be definitely decided in Stockholm, is the definition of the zone in which CSBMs were to be applicable.

(a) *The Zone of Application*

The provisions of the Helsinki Final Act represent a rough balance between the security interests of the 35 states of Europe and North America. This is true of all sections of the document, including the chapter entitled "Document on Confidence-Building Measures and Certain

---

[47]*Decisions of the Helsinki Preparatory Meeting, op. cit.*, p. 4. See Appendix.

Aspects of Security and Disarmament." Any changes in these provisions inevitably require the specification of a new balance. This was above all the case with the territorial zone delineated in the Final Act. The point of departure for defining the zone was the formula adopted in the Helsinki Final Act with reference to notification to be given when they are to take place "on the territory, in Europe, of any participating State as well as, if applicable, in the adjoining sea area and air space."[48] However, the Final Act qualified this obligation in the case of states whose territory extends beyond Europe — i.e., the USSR and Turkey — by saying that they need give notification only of those major maneuvers "which take place in an area within 250 kilometers from its frontier facing any other European participating State." One can therefore distinguish in the CSCE Final Act between three different categories of states from the point of view of confidence-building measures in the military sphere:

- states whose territory is not covered by these measures (USA, Canada);

- states whose territory is partly covered by them (USSR, Turkey);

- other European states whose territory is entirely subject to the measures agreed on at Helsinki.

The idea put forward at Madrid by the Western states that CSBMs should be applicable to the whole European territory of the USSR ("from the Atlantic to the Urals") was found acceptable by the Soviet Union, on the understanding, however, that the Western countries would make a corresponding extension in the geographical scope of these measures on their side.[49] The expected trade-off was chiefly a matter of including sea and ocean areas (the North Atlantic) in the CSBM zone, the point being that the naval forces, particularly the American fleet, deployed in this region form an important part of the overall military balance in Europe. The military activity involved is not immaterial to the state of security in Europe and cannot be bypassed in the application of CSBMs.

At first, in view of the unwillingness of the West to accede to the Soviet demand, the USSR suggested adoption of a general formula with regard to this question at Madrid, to be followed by the elaboration of a

---

[48]*Encyclopedia of the United Nations and International Agreements, op.cit.*, p. 335.

[49]The Soviet position was presented publicly on February 23, 1981, in Leonid Brezhnev's report to the 26th CPSU Congress.

more specific definition of the zone at the Stockholm Conference. The United States delegation vetoed this solution and came up instead with what it called a "functional" approach to the CSBM zone. Essentially, this amounted to the restrictive interpretation of the relevant CSCE provision introduced by the U.S. delegate at Geneva on July 19, 1975 in a unilateral reservation to the draft of the Final Act, which held that none of the clauses in the section dealing with major military maneuvers could be held to apply to independent or combined naval and air exercises.[50] Under this approach CSBMs would be applicable only to military activity on land, the sea areas adjoining the continent being included only in the case of operations which formed an integral part of notified military activity involving land forces. In other words, the only sea and air activity subject to the CSBM regime would be that functionally connected with land-based maneuvers or other land operations. The American rejection of the Soviet *quid pro quo* demand became the principal cause of the prolonged deadlock in the negotiations on the Concluding Document of the Madrid Meeting.

The delineation of the CSBM zone adopted in the Concluding Document of the Madrid Meeting represents a compromise. According to the Document, the zone will "cover the whole of Europe as well as the adjoining sea areas and air space." The Document states that the measures will be applicable to military activities "whenever these activities affect security in Europe as well as constitute a part of activities taking place within the whole of Europe...."

In the official American assessment, the extension of the area to the Urals was correctly defined as "quite significant." On the other hand, the Soviet idea of extending the geographical area into the north Atlantic Ocean as compensation for its extension to the Ural Mountains cannot be rejected simply by referring to "the freedom of the high seas". This is so because the CSCE conferences in Helsinki, Madrid and Stockholm were and are concerned with the problem of *security in Europe.* This can by no means be reduced to military activities on the European continent. The problem of surprise military attack cannot be reduced to land activity only and should also encompass the surveillance and observation of naval forces, including submarines, aircraft and other

---

[50]Journal No. 246/bis, CSCE I/1, Geneva, July 19, 1975. For more details see Rotfeld (ed.), *From Helsinki to Madrid. CSCE Documents, op. cit.,* p. 34.

instruments of surprise attack deployed at sea and in the air, as stipulated by the Western experts at the 1958 Geneva Surprise Attack Conference.[51]

(b) *Degree of Commitment*

Decisions to be taken in Stockholm will be "politically binding". The nature of this CSCE resolution is not clear. Jurists hold the traditional view that only legal norms need be treated as obligatory in international relations. All other norms — of a political or moral nature — enjoy no such status. The problem, however, is that the CSCE decisions are meant to serve as an instrument of political action, in the sphere of politics, security, economics, in humanitarian and other fields, which cannot necessarily be identified with the spheres regulated by international law. This distinction clearly appears in the text of the Final Act. Principal 10 ("Fulfillment in Good Faith of Obligations under International Law") states:

> In exercising their sovereign rights, including the right to determine their laws and regulations, they (the participating States) will conform with their legal obligations under international law; they will furthermore pay due regard to and implement the provisions in the Final Act of the Conference on Security and Co-operation in Europe.[52]

The unique character of the CSCE decisions, then, stems not from oversight but from the deliberate political will of the states concerned. The main aim of the parties involved in the negotiations was not to create a new legal instrument but rather to construct effective political machinery. These general considerations fully apply to the mandate of the Stockholm Conference.

This introduced a new element into the military aspects of European security discussed in the CSCE process. The set of CBMs provided by the Helsinki Final Act is of a voluntary nature. In addition, the degree of commitment was differentiated for each measure: for notification of major maneuvers the operational word "*will* be given" was used; for other smaller manuevers, "*may.*" Exchange of invitations to observers "*will*" be given, but "voluntarily and on a bilateral basis, in a spirit of

---

[51]U.S. Dept. of State, *Documents on Disarmament 1945-1959, op. cit.*, vol. II, doc. 319, 324, *passim.*

[52]*Encyclopedia of the United Nations and International Agreements, op. cit.*, p. 334.

reciprocity and goodwill"; for the notification of major military movements the formula was used that the states *may* do so "at their own discretion."[53] In contrast to the vagueness of the Final Act provisions, the mandate for Stockholm means that all decisions to be taken there will be binding. Yet this raises a complication. The broader the scope of the zone and the greater the obligations thereby imposed, the less the chance of meeting the very ambitious requirements tabled by the NATO countries in Stockholm.

(c) *"Military Significance"*

The demand for "militarily significant" measures was connected chiefly with the conviction that CBMs in the Final Act did not improve the political-military situation because they were too modest and of a political and psychological, rather than a military, character. By definition this expression in the Mandate is relative and therefore ambiguous.

First, the obligations considered as militarily insignificant for one country or group of countries may be of great importance for another one. The extreme example is connected with the CSBMs regime for military activities in the adjoining sea and air space, which, while irrelevant for non-coastal countries (like Austria, Czechoslovakia, Hungary or Switzerland) are of utmost significance for the countries whose military security is based in large measure on naval and air forces (the great powers, typical coastal countries like Greece and Turkey, Cyprus, Portugal, etc.). Second, the same obligations in different times and circumstances may be considered as significant or insignificant, depending on changes in political and military interests.

Now, the proposals tabled in Stockholm by the NATO countries focus on problems of exhange of military information, forecasts of activities notifiable in advance, pre-notification of military exercises, observation, verification and communication. All of these measures considered by the Western countries as militarily significant could be put in the category of information and verification; whereas for the Soviet Union and the other WTO countries measures of genuine military significance are represented first of all by the prohibition, reduction, limitation and

[53]For more, see Rotfeld, "CBMs between Helsinki and Madrid," in Larrabee and Stobbe (eds.), *op. cit.*, pp. 89-99.

constraint on military activities, including production, deployment, and use, as well as by the new specific undertaking regarding the effectiveness of the principle of non-use of force (both nuclear and conventional).

The main task for the negotiators in Stockholm is to find a balance and common denominator between these two approaches, including the expectations of the group of N/NA states. This means in practice that the NATO countries should take into account the legitimate security interests of their partners without identifying the new generations of CSBMs with the improvement of what are inevitably seen as intelligence-gathering possibilities and imposing this understanding as the only common concept of East-West confidence-building.

(d) *Forms of Verification*

New CSBMs, according to the Mandate, "will be provided with adequate forms of verification which correspond to their content." In Stockholm, three categories of confidence-building measures are being negotiated and most probably will be adopted: military-political (non-use of force), informational (notification and observation), and constraint measures (limitations on activities and deployment). Forms of verification should be subordinated to each of them. Verification is not considered in the mandate as an independent measure. The group of N/NA states proposed jointly to accept this approach.[54] In fact, the approach of the N/NA countries in this respect is indicative. For them an agreement at Stockholm could bring about qualitative changes in their access to military information (since, for the time being, this group of countries possesses rather limited national means of verification), while for the U.S. and some NATO states "the information provided would be no different from that already gained by Western 'national-technical means'."[55]

The functions of verification can be seen in three categories:

- to minimize the frictions connected with CSBM compliance;
- to secure the mutual reassurance for East and West that a surprise attack in Europe is out of the question (warning);
- to remove the sources of tensions in crisis situations (an element of crisis management).

---

[54]CSCE/SC.3, Stockholm, March 9, 1984.
[55]Darilek, *op. cit.*, p. 133.

Verification per se does not produce confidence. What is more, a distorted understanding of CSBMs, which are seen sometimes exclusively as instruments of verification, is counterproductive because questioning the good intentions of a partner is itself a new cause of mistrust and tension. In other words, verification should be considered as functionally related and subordinated to substantive, militarily significant arms control and confidence-building measures.

Since one of the basic aims of CSBMs is the proper interpretation of military intentions, the question arises: How can one verify the intentions behind large-scale military activities? By access to numerical data? By the elaboration of sophisticated technical arrangements? By the establishment of special mechanisms of inspection or channels of communication? The adequate form and scope of verification can only be established in relation to compliance with the specific set of CSBMs to be produced by the Stockholm Conference.

The creation of new multilateral institutions toward this end within the framework of the CSCE and Stockholm Conference seems, at the present stage of East-West relations, improbable. In fact, many suggestions tabled in Stockholm under the rubric of exchange of military information, exchange of forecasts of activities notifiable in advance, as well as notification and observation of military activities and development of means of communications, would constitute mechanisms of compliance and verification far beyond the content of an actual measure.[56] Therefore, specific monitoring and verification measures proposed by the sixteen NATO sponsors appear to be aimed at reducing CSBMs solely to a surveillance function rather than elaborating adequate forms of verification that will correspond to the content of adopted confidence-building measures.[57] Excessive verification demands will create new sources of distrust in the negotiation process and therefore hinder the establishment of a new CSBM system.

---

[56]CSCE/SC.1, *Working Documents I, II, III, IV and V,* tabled in Stockholm on January 30, February 7, 12, 14 and 27, 1985.

[57]CSCE/SC.1 *Working Document V,* Stockholm, February 20, 1985.

(e) Aims and Basic Assumptions

The mandate negotiated in Madrid explicitly states that the aim of the Conference is to embark by stages on new, effective and concrete steps in the process of strengthening confidence and security and bringing about disarmament in Europe. Progress in this direction entails giving teeth to the binding principle outlawing the use or threat of force in international relations.

The Stockholm Conference should be seen, on the one hand, as an essential and integral part of the CSCE process and, on the other, as an attempt to add a new dimension to this process and its influence on the sphere of military relations. The first stage of the Stockholm Conference, which began on January 17, 1984, is, as was decided at Madrid, "devoted to the negotiation and adoption of a set of mutually complementary CSBMs designed to reduce the risk of military confrontation in Europe." Behind this decision lay the assumption that progress on simpler issues would clear the way to tackling more difficult and complex problems, such as disarmament. The mandate states that decisions at Stockholm are to be taken "on the basis of equality of rights, balance and reciprocity, equal respect for the security interests of all the CSCE participating States, and of their respective obligations concerning CSBMs in Europe...." The task of the Stockholm Conference is to give concrete shape to these general guidelines by translating them into practical obligations.

2. The Negotiating Positions at Stockholm

Exaggerated hopes and expectations usually lead to disappointment. The proceedings at Stockholm were bound to be affected by the fact that they coincided with the deployment of new American medium-range missiles in Europe. The delegations of the socialist countries therefore stressed the need to desist from any steps or action which might jeopardize the purpose of the talks in question.

The attendance of the inaugural session of the Conference by the foreign ministers of the Warsaw Treaty, NATO, neutral and non-aligned states indicates that both East and West attached great political significance to the Stockholm proceedings, testimony to the viability of the structures of detente established by the CSCE. The keynote and common theme of the majority of speeches from East and West were both a declared will to continue the process begun at Helsinki and extend it to the sphere of military relations, and an emphasis on new dangers and the urgent necessity of gradual deescalation of political and military tensions. Measures and instruments are being sought which would make it possible to recover control over a situation perilously drifting towards war. What is needed here are not new accusations, but concrete and practical steps and arrangements, modest and limited as they may be. The negotiating positions assumed at Stockholm reflect, of course, the broader attitudes and diverse political philosophies that govern the approaches to military security of the main actors on the European stage.

(a) *The NATO Position*

The United States and its NATO allies are pressing for measures that would increase the quantity and range of information relating to armed forces and their activity and the verifiability of such data. This approach is exemplified by the proposal submitted by the NATO states at Stockholm on January 24, 1984, and one year later in the form of working documents tabled in February 1985, in which the means of information, transparency, observation and verification become an end in themselves.[58] Their adoption in a time of tension would lead, the Warsaw Treaty states argue, to a growth of threats and a war psychosis.

A general assessment of the six-point NATO proposals was made by the Soviet delegation during the initial rounds of the Stockholm Conference.[59] The main point, according to the head of the Soviet delegation, was that the NATO document

> totally overlooks the key issues of strengthening peace and security in Europe, narrows the possibilities of the Conference, reduces the business at the Conference to secondary military and technical matters and does not envisage any limitation of military activities. The NATO approach makes an unwarranted hyperbole of the verification issue in total isolation from the content of the confidence-building measures.[60]

The first point of the NATO proposal suggests the exchange of detailed data on the structure of ground forces and land-based air forces

---

[58]CSCE/SC.1 and six working documents tabled between January 30 and February 27, 1985 in Stockholm compiled in SC.1/Amplified, Stockholm, March 8, 1985 (see Appendix).

[59]See for example, the statements of the Soviet delegation in Stockholm on January 29, March 1, March 8 and 16, and May 8, 1984.

[60]Statement by Amb. Oleg Grinevsky, Stockholm, June 20, 1984.

in the zone of application for agreed CSBMs. The annually exchanged information would encompass the military command organization of each country and its regulations for accredited military personnel. This information would include the following elements:

- Composition of ground and land-based air forces (ground formations and main combat units as well as land-based air formations).

- The exchange of annual forecasts of activities notifiable in advance — if adopted — would provide for each calendar year, on a quarterly basis, specific information not only about the designation and general purpose of activity but also, on a thirty-day basis, the geographic coordinates, the number of troops and the type of forces that will be engaged, etc.

- Pre-notification would cover: all out-of-garrison activities in the zone (on the level of one or more ground-force divisions or 6,000 or more ground troops not organized into a division); mobilization activities (when 25,000 or more troops of three or more divisions are involved); amphibious activities (three battalions or 3,000 amphibious troops); and alert activities.

The other measures proposed by the NATO countries concern the various elements of notification, observation, compliance and verification, and the development of communication. In accordance with the NATO document, each of the 35 CSCE participating states would be permitted "to inspect a military activity or possible military activity within the zone for the purpose of monitoring compliance with agreed CSBMs."[61] The intent of the sponsors is made clear in the declaration that "any possible dispute as to the validity of this citation will not prevent or delay the conduct of an inspection." The inspection would proceed within 12 hours after the issuance of an inspection request. The inspectors would be granted "those diplomatic privileges and immunities necessary to enable them to perform their tasks fully and unhindered at all times."

In the Soviet understanding this kind of expectation encroaches upon the *sancta sanctorum* of every European state, i.e., upon the field of its security. The main Soviet objections are connected with the fact that the NATO countries are proposing intrusive measures, addressed mainly to the Soviet Union and other WTO states, "while the U.S.," in Soviet

---

[61]CSCE/SC.1/Amplified, Stockholm, March 8, 1985.

Ambassador Oleg Grinevsky's words, "does not intend to apply these measures to a single inch of its own territory." Such an approach, in Grinevsky's assessment of the NATO position, unfortunately creates unilateral advantages and provides NATO with a cover in order to enhance the military activity of naval forces (mainly U.S.).[62] In order to reconcile the principle of equality of rights, balance, reciprocity and respect for equal security interests with the exclusion of the main American forces stationed overseas, but first of all the exclusion of the forces with missiles and aircraft deployed in the sea areas and air space adjoining Europe, the Western countries should display a more cooperative approach in other issues under negotiation in Stockholm.

The Stockholm Conference cannot be artificially limited to issues of ground forces and land activities. In the mandate there are no concrete indications or limitations as to the specific content of confidence- and security-building measures to be examined. So, *any* undertaking which can contribute to the removal of existing fears and distrust and correspond to accepted criteria is appropriate for consideration. Moreover, the intention expressed in the mandate to aim at "mutually complementary measures" requires a comprehensive approach to the subject of negotiations.

(b) *The WTO Position*

The approach of the Soviet Union and other Warsaw Treaty countries to CSBMs was determined from the very beginning by the deterioration of the military situation and by the increased risk of military confrontation in Europe. The continuing deployment of new American missiles in Western Europe was viewed as the main factor undermining confidence and security inside and outside of Europe. Therefore, the WTO has wanted CSBMs that would facilitate the prevention of nuclear war, limit military activity and so give more concrete shape to the principle of non-use of force. Such measures should be adequate for their purpose, i.e., to reduce the danger of surprise attack or the outbreak of armed conflict as a result of accident or misinterpretation. This aim would be better served by a decrease in military activities than by the most sophisticated mechanism of surveillance, monitoring and verification.

---

[62]*Ibid.*

Without denying the need to extend the catalogue and range of confidence-building measures envisaged by the Helsinki Final Act, the Soviet Union and its allies nevertheless accord priority to the conclusion of agreements of a military and political nature. "To confine ourselves in this area to a single direction," then Soviet Foreign Minister Andrei Gromyko said in Stockholm on January 18, 1984, "would amount to narrowing the existing possibilities."[63] The WTO countries take the view that a serious approach to confidence- and security-building requires the adoption of measures that would eliminate the possiblity of war breaking out in Europe. Soviet representatives in Stockholm have argued that these should include:

- a no-first-use obligation by all nuclear states (a no-first-use agreement would embrace all 35 CSCE states: NATO, WTO, and N/NA countries);

- the conclusion of an agreement on the non-use of military force (i.e., renunciation of the use of conventional as well as nuclear weapons);

- an agreement on the reduction of military expenditures;

- the establishment in Europe of a chemical weapons-free zone;

- creation of regional nuclear-free zones in Europe (e.g., Northern Europe and the Balkans);

- a new series of CSBMs going beyond those contained in the Helsinki Final Act.

The Warsaw Treaty states also expressed their willingness to alter, as the West has suggested, some of the parameters relating to the measures agreed upon in the CSCE Final Act. Specifically, this concerns prior notification of planned maneuvers, major troop movements and transfer of forces. The socialist countries have also recommended lowering the ceiling of exercises to a limited number of troops (20,000). They also favor prior notification of major air and naval exercises in the waters and air space surrounding Europe. Inclusion of pre-notification and observation of specified air and naval activities is intended, in the WTO view, to restore a balance of interests and facilitate compromise by avoiding sterile disputes on the definition of the zone of application.

---

[63]CSCE/SC/PR. 3, p. 30.

Toward this end the Polish delegation, on February 10, 1986, advanced a proposal which defines in detail the procedure of inviting observers as well as the terms and manner of their functioning. The proposal also delineates the rights and responsibilities of observers. The essence of the proposal consists in creating a relationship between notification of military activity and its observation. It is thereby designed to answer the concern about demonstrating the peaceful intentions of the inviting state and confirming the compliance of monitored activity with previous notification. The Polish document thus exemplifies the principle of taking into consideration the interests and views of all parties to the negotiations.

That the Warsaw Treaty states are very much interested in achieving a meaningful agreement at Stockholm was demonstrated in a series of statements by Soviet General Secretary Mikhail S. Gorbachev in late 1985-early 1986. Responding to the discernible thaw in the international political climate as the November 1985 Geneva summit with the U.S. approached, the Soviet Union initiated a search for areas where rapid progress toward East-West accords was feasible. The Stockholm Conference was very high on the list. In his address to the French National Assembly in October 1985, for instance, Gorbachev underlined the need to strike a balance between military-technical measures and political CBMs in Stockholm. Gorbachev declared the USSR's willingness to "make more concrete and impart maximum effectiveness to the principle of the non-use of force." In addition, he continued, an agreement in Stockholm should

> include a specific set of confidence-building measures in the military field, these "safety fuses" to prevent an erroneous interpretation of the actions of the other side in conditions of an aggravation of the military confrontation.... We are prepared...to reach agreement on mutual exchanges of annual plans of military activity subject to notification.[64]

In his comprehensive disarmament proposal of January 15, 1986, Gorbachev went further, and, in reference to the CDE, called for removing the issue of naval forces as an immediate bone of contention in Stockholm. A key obstacle to progress in the talks was thereby removed. Gorbachev said:

---

[64]*Pravda,* October 4, 1985, p. 2.

> The time has come to undertake at the conference the solution of unsolved problems. As is known, the narrowest bottleneck is the matter of notifying large-scale exercises of the army, navy and air forces.
>
> ...If, however, it proves impossible to solve these problems in a comprehensive way, why not try to find partial solutions for the time being? Say, to reach an agreement now as concerns notifying large-scale exercises of the army and air forces, and to postpone the matter of naval activities to the next stage of the conference.[65]

Furthermore, the USSR has since the fall of 1985 dropped its insistence that an agreement on the non-use of force be included in treaty form.[66] A politically binding reaffirmation of the principle is now satisfactory to the USSR and the other Warsaw Treaty states. In spite of the often sharply conflicting views of the NATO and WTO sides in Stockholm, then, it is very possible to reach an agreement on the main issues, provided that both sides manifest a will to take each other's security interests and perspectives into account. The Warsaw Treaty states have indicated their desire to do so.

(c) *The Romanian Position*

Measures proposed by Romania at the Stockholm Conference were aimed at the elimination of suspicions and the sense of insecurity caused by military activities; the diminution, restraint and limitation of military activities in border areas; and the extension of information, communication and consultations between states, especially in crisis situations.

The geographical and numerical limits on military activities suggested by Romania were associated with a change in parameters providing for notification and the establishment of new demilitarized zones (e.g., a corridor free of nuclear and other weapons of mass destruction along the borders of NATO and WTO states) and some other constraint measures: nuclear weapons-free zones in the Balkans and in northern Europe, and a freeze of foreign troops, foreign bases and military expenditures. Certain ideas (i.e., a non-use of force treaty) and parameters proposed by Romania were

---

[65]*Statement by Mikhail Gorbachev, General Secretary of the CPSU Central Committee, January 15, 1986* (Moscow: Novosti, 1986), p. 12.

[66]See *Ibid.*, in which the entire discussion on creating "barriers to the use of force" is in terms of militarily specific CSBMs. Gorbachev does not even mention a treaty on the non-use of force.

consistent with the recommendations tabled by the Soviet Union and some of those suggested by the neutral and non-aligned countries.

(d) *Position of the N/NA Countries*

The group of neutral and non-aligned states (N/NA) presented proposals on March 9, 1984 and November 15, 1985, reflecting their own aspirations. These were not compromise documents. The N/NA suggested extension and improvement of the CBMs specified in the Final Act and the introduction of a number of qualitatively new measures which to some extent overlap with the thrust of the NATO proposals. The N/NA states have drawn attention to the need to subordinate these measures to the broader concept of non-use of force and elements of restraint (e.g., limitation of the size of major maneuvers). These are treated as preliminary steps toward tackling the problem of disarmament in the second stage of the Conference.[67]

The first N/NA document also contained a general and vague formulation about the "creation of conditions for considering" a reaffirmation, in appropriate ways and forms, of the duty of states to refrain from the threat or use of force in their mutual relations. The idea of non-use of force was mentioned in a joint paragraph together with the commitment to the peaceful settlement of disputes. The language of both N/NA documents intentionally leaves open the possibility for this group of countries to play an active role in search of compromise in the latter stage of negotiations. This will, however, prove more difficult than in the past since, as measures (such as constraints on military activities) touch more directly on central concerns of national security, it will prove more difficult for such a diverse group as the N/NA countries to find a militarily significant common ground. An earlier, separate document tabled by Malta adapted all the measures (of information, notification, restraint, observation and verification, as well as measures of security) to the specific requirements of the Mediterranean and was concerned mainly with naval activities.[68]

---

[67]CSCE/SC.3, Stockholm, March 9, 1984, and CSCE/SC.7, November 15, 1985, respectively (see Appendix).

[68]CSCE/SC.5, Stockholm, November 8, 1984.

3. Assessment of Negotiations

The course of the initial discussions at the Stockholm Conference closely reflected the state of East-West relations. The NATO states sought a technical debate and were anxious to avoid political assessments of the new situation. The WTO countries, on the other hand, regarded the conference as an opportunity to explore the concept of CSBMs in a broader politico-military context. These differences spring from dissimilar perceptions of the aims and tasks of the Stockholm Conference. For the NATO delegates it is a meeting of experts whose job is to discuss detailed technical problems. The WTO countries see it as a forum which ought to address the key issues involved in reducing the military confrontation in Europe. In fact, CSBMs form part of a larger whole. They can fulfill the hopes attached to them only if they are made a fundamental element in the construction of a system of common security for the whole of Europe. The participants in the Stockholm Conference are thus confronted with a dilemma: whether to make a routine search for the lowest common denominator in the development of technical-military measures alone or whether to face up to the challenge of the times and explore long-term solutions that would give Europe a sense of genuine stability and security commensurate with current dangers.

(a) *The Military-Technical Approach*

The advocates of the military-technical approach to CSBMs ascribe a major role to confidence-building measures aimed at increased openness, transparency, and predictability. Such measures boil down to steps aimed at broadening information, notification, observation and verification. In keeping with this approach, CBMs should reflect the military situation and not influence or shape it.

Falk Bomsdorf, a member of the UN experts group on CBMs, has argued that the differences between Eastern and Western interpretations of CBMs are connected not only with the different meaning of the word "confidence", but also with the ambiguous understanding of the term "measure":

> When talking of a confidence-building measure, the West means a concrete action which can be verified and evaluated. Only concrete actions — so the argument runs — may provide evidence for the absence of feared threats. The East does not restrict itself to this meaning of "measure". On the contrary, it also includes among "confidence-building measures" moves which are not concrete actions but declarations. Declarations, however, cannot be

verified or evaluated; you can only believe in them or not. A declaration
on the renunciation of the use of force, for example, can either be trusted
or not; it gives no indication whatever of the absence of a military threat.[69]

In fact, the problem is much more complicated than the simple juxta-
position of "concrete" vs. "declaratory" measures. Political and military
confidence cannot be reduced to the exchange of information about the
number of troops or observation of military maneuvers. Political steps,
taken with the aim of dispelling mistrust, are much more important than
new parameters of notification, observation or verification.

This kind of thinking was dominant ten years ago in Geneva and
Helsinki. It also found reflection in the CSCE Final Act. One could even
say — leaving aside the modest scope of the CBMs contained in the Final
Act — that they had no real bearing on military relations in Europe. They
have neither curbed military activity to any extent nor have they had any
effect on reducing the military confrontation in East-West relations. Most
likely, this state of affairs would not have been changed by other proposed
parameters concerning notification. Thus, for example, more detailed
and timely information on NATO's "Central Enterprise 84" or "Distant
Hammer 84" maneuvers would have had no impact on the objective or
scope of these exercises. In addition, an invitation offered in a tense
situation characterized by mutual suspicion and growing lack of trust might
well be interpreted as an attempt at increasing the intimidating effect of
the demonstration of power. This does not mean that the passive function
of such CSBMs as the exchange of information, mutual notification,
observation and verification cannot favorably influence the development
of East-West relations or the proper perception of military activity and
the elimination of threats stemming from misunderstanding and erroneous
assessments. There is a danger, however, that an excessive stress put
on this function of CSBMs may produce unintended consequences: a war
psychosis and an enhanced sense of threat, which in a tense atmosphere
might heighten rather than scale down the level of military confrontation.
Moreover, it might divert attention away from the need to modify the
present military situation and shape a new system of political-military
relations in Europe.

---

[69]Falk Bomsdorf, "The Third World, Europe and Confidence-Building Measures," in Hugh
Haning (ed.), *Peacekeeping and Confidence-Building Measures in the Third World*
(New York: International Peace Academy, 1985), p. 40.

(b) *The Political-Military Approach*

The political-military approach to CSBMs views confidence-building measures in a wider political and military context. According to Johan Holst, the Stockholm Conference creates a framework for negotiations and dialogue "about concrete measures which could contribute in the short term towards the construction of a more secure political order in Europe." In the long run this opens the possibility of shaping a new situation in Europe, which would be characterized by "greater equity and stability". Such measures, Holst writes, "should be designed to enhance security by providing mechanisms for mutual reassurance."[70] Existing mechanisms of national security, or security within the framework of existing alliances, are not conducive to such reassurance. "Security in the nuclear age," Holst thus concludes, "is also common security with the unavoidable corollary that states must exercise mutual restraint."[71]

Measures of information, as well as observation and verification measures, by their very nature have an impact mainly on the *perception* of military activity; they have a bearing, above all, on the explanation of intentions by which other partners guide themselves in developing their military activity. Yet as Holst correctly notes, tension and conflicts of interest between East and West are not "only, or even primarily, the result of misperception and misunderstanding or cognitive dissonance."[72]

The weakness of "passive" CSBMs is that, at most, such measures can only register facts. They are not intended to have any bearing on the scope, integrity, or frequency of military activity and so cannot affect the actual sources of military tensions in Europe. Such a conception of CSBMs (erroneously) presupposes that confidentiality of military information is dictated mainly by aggressive designs. Numerous examples both from past and present illustrate that, on the contrary, military secrecy is often the weapon of the weaker side, which serves to disguise various loopholes and shortages in its defensive system. On the other hand, broad information on increased military activity, e.g., programs of intensified armaments, data on introduction of new types and systems of weapons, various demonstrations of military power, etc., may lead to

---

[70]Johan J. Holst, "Confidence and Security in Europe: A Long-Term View," *Bulletin of Peace Proposals*, vol. 15, no. 4, 1984, p. 291.

[71]*Ibid.*, p. 292.

[72]*Ibid.*, p. 291.

the exertion of political and military pressure on a specific state or group of states and the weakening of the resolve and capacity of their defense in the face of a real or simulated superiority; in other words, to the attainment of political goals indirectly, without outright resort to armed force. In present conditions this is precisely the chief function of atomic weapons.

Limiting the development of CSBMs to this passive function thus may add to the further militarization of international relations rather than to an increased sense of security. That is why particular attention should be paid to those measures and actions that can contribute to decreasing the role of the military factor and to an improvement of relations between East and West. In this category one should include above all the set of measures that would promote military restraint by states.

(c) *Restraint Measures*

The notion of restraint includes all agreed or tacit, unilateral, bilateral or multilateral measures aimed at decreasing the military activity or military presence of states. Such measures — whether stemming from a political decision or based on internationally valid agreements — may have a limited scope of operation as regards their subject and object; they may refer to a specific type of military activity or to a specific type of armament; finally, they may be limited in time and geographic focus.

As indicated above, a number of constraint measures have been advanced by WTO countries since the adoption of the Helsinki Final Act in 1975. These include possible agreements on no-first-use of nuclear weapons and on the non-use of force, reduction of military expenditures, the establishment of chemical-weapons and nuclear weapons-free zones in Europe, and various limitations on military maneuvers and movements and other activities in Europe.

Constraint measures are designed to introduce changes in military posture and military behavior and thus limit the possibility of war, without decreasing the material stocks necessary to ensure the security of states within the framework of the existing balance of forces. Criticism of such constraint measures usually comes down to the charge that these proposals are of a "declaratory and progaganda" nature. This refers especially to the postulate concerning the adoption of obligations on no-first-use and on the conclusion of an agreement on the non-use of military force. As regards the latter, it has long been argued that there is no need to conclude a new agreement on the non-use of force, since:

(a) the United Nations Charter is in force, which provides for such a ban in terms of international law and in practice has a universally binding character; and

(b) this ban has been reiterated both in the UN Declaration of 1970 concerning the principles of international law and in the Declaration on the principles of the CSCE, as well as in numerous bilateral and multilateral political and legal acts. Conclusion of a new agreement, critics maintain, would not strengthen, but weaken the effectiveness of a ban on the use of force.

These arguments are more of a tactical than a substantive nature. Such doubts were not raised, e.g., when the FRG advanced a proposal on the renunciation of the use of force with regard to its Eastern neighbors; conclusion of such accords became possible when the reasons that might encourage the use of force were eliminated. Thus, renunciation of force was accompanied by the renunciation of territorial claims and revision of frontiers once and for all.

Adoption of an obligation on a reciprocal basis in any form (in a legal or non-legal document), on the non-use of military force (both nuclear and conventional) by all CSCE states would stabilize the situation in Europe and increase the feeling of security among all the participants in such an agreement. The agreement might include a number of obligations that would meet the reservations expressed by those critical of such an undertaking. That is why it is necessary to undertake multilateral consultations, which would examine the general idea as well as its specific elements (e.g., the relation between new obligations and the provisions included in the UN Charter, CSCE Final Act and other bilateral and multilateral international documents).

In fact, the CSCE Final Act explicitly recommends making the principle of the non-use of force more effective. The Final Act obligates the participating states "to give effect and expression by all the ways and forms which they consider appropriate, to the duty to refrain from the threat or use of force in their relations with one another." The essence of the Soviet concept submitted in Stockholm is not the simple reiteration or reaffirmation of an idea already embodied in the UN Charter or Helsinki Final Act; rather, it is intended to make that idea more concrete and specific, to develop and adapt it to the realities of Europe, as has been done with other principles expressed in the UN Charter (e.g., in favor of human rights, against racial discrimination, etc.). This is all the more true as Article 52 of the UN Charter envisages the conclusion of regional agreements for dealing with such matters relating to the maintenance of international peace and security "as are appropriate for regional action." The position of the NATO countries is, apparently, evolving. A change was signaled in President Ronald Reagan's speech in Dublin on June 4, 1984, where he said:

> If discussions on reaffirming the principle not to use force, a principle in which we believe so deeply, will bring the Soviet Union to negotiate agreements which will give concrete new meaning to that principle, we will gladly enter into such discussions.[73]

One year later, speaking before the West European Parliament in Strasbourg (May 8, 1985), President Reagan submitted the concept of "a military-to-military communications link," a kind of bilateral Soviet-American CBM. He declared U.S. readiness "to discuss the Soviet proposal on non-use of force in the context of Soviet agreement to concrete confidence-building measures."[74] Unfortunately, the president's speeches did not soon lead to a significant change in the posture of the NATO delegations at the Stockholm negotiations, which — considering the time constraints on the negotiators — led to a number of lost opportunities at the conference.

On May 11, 1985 the Romanian delegation produced an aide-memoire suggesting the initiation of formal and informal consultations with a view to identifying those elements "which could form a package of substantive and balanced CSBMs able to constitute the outline of a future agreement." The Romanian document indicated some areas of convergence that could be considered as components of a compromise agreement for the first stage of the Stockholm Conference:

1. The non-use of force obligation could be dealt with in a "solemn declaration" (as proposed by Cyprus on March 8, 1985).

2. Simultaneously, a set of measures would be introduced that "would give effect and expression to the duty of States to refrain from the threat or use of force in their mutual relations" (from the mandate of the Stockholm Conference). In this context the Romanian aide-memoire referred to the following CSBMs:

---

[73] *Weekly Compilation of Presidential Documents*, June 4, 1984, p. 833.

[74] *The New York Times*, May 9, 1985.

- binding notification of military activities (including "a mutual exchange of annual forecasts of notifiable military activities");
- invitation of observers from all participating states ("to those notifiable military activities which by their size and area of deployment could generate suspicions and insecurity to other States");
- limitation of forces engaged in major military maneuvers and of the duration and number of such exercises;
- the establishment of procedures and channels for information, communication and consultations (for example, establishment of special telephone and telex connections, exchange of military delegations, exchange of information on national regulations regarding the accredited military personnel and — under extreme circumstances — establishment of fact-finding missions).

Those proposals which could not be incorporated into the decisions of the first stage would continue to be subject to negotiation in the second stage. At present, the Stockholm negotiations are focused on five topics, which should be reflected in the Final Document of the Conference:

- embodiment of the principle of the non-use of force;
- exchange of military information, verification, consultation and expansion of means of communication;
- exchange of annual plans of military activity and limitation of certain types of this activity;
- notification;
- observation of military activity.

Agreement within the framework suggested here would create the initial preconditions for arms limitations and reductions. As a rule the structure of negotiations tends to shape the final outcome. In the case of the Stockholm Conference, the structure assures equal treatment of all tabled proposals.[75] The N/NA countries showed their interest in a positive outcome for the Stockholm Conference by a number of political statements and by an active search for areas of potential consensus. These areas were outlined in an extension and qualitative improvement of the notification and observation measures contained in the Helsinki Final Act.

---

[75]*CSCE/SC, Journal*, No. 117 from 123rd Plenary Meeting. See also Karl E. Birnbaum, "The First Year of the Stockholm Conference," *SIPRI Yearbook 1985*, p. 535.

Room for eventual consensus can be seen in the question of non-use of force. Possibilities for developing measures of constraint have also been explored. Speaking on behalf of Finland, Undersecretary of State Klaus Tornudd expressed the view that the establishment of nuclear weapons-free zones "may be regarded as significant confidence-building measures."[76] A number of other delegations shared this reasoning. An encouraging note regarding the eventual conclusion of an agreement on the non-use of force at Stockholm was struck at the U.S.-Soviet summit in November 1985, at which both leaders, in their joint statement, said that the Stockholm document should provide for confidence- and security-building measures acceptable for both sides as well as the embodiment of the principle of the non-use of force and making it effective. As noted earlier, the precise form in which the non-use of force principle is embedded — legally binding treaty or political declaration — is now a moot issue.

While CSBMs cannot substitute for disarmament, they may greatly facilitate it. This can come about not if negotiators approach CSBMs as measures designed to bring short-term benefits for any single state or group of states, but rather as elements of a long-term process intended to construct a system of common and equal security for all.

[76]Statement by Finnish Undersecretary of State Klaus Tornudd, Stockholm, March 15, 1985.

III.

Conclusion

European Security and CSBMs

1. Security, in the nuclear age, is not to be confused with the absence of war. Security today embraces more complex and broader dimensions of various military and non-military factors. We are speaking of a new situation, without precedent in the history of mankind, which demands qualitatively new solutions adequate to the new threats. The contemporary paradox was accurately captured by Albert Einstein after the explosion of the first atomic bomb when he observed that the bomb had changed everything but the way man thinks. In the nuclear age security can be assured not simply by new military technologies but in the first instance by political measures. Only international agreement can provide the foundations for security.

2. Europe — in the context of security deliberations — cannot be considered only as a geographical notion. The CSCE was not a conference on geography but on security and cooperation in Europe. The security of Europe can be affected by military activities taking place on the sea and ocean areas adjoining it. Consequently, as the result of the negotiations in Madrid, the notion of military activities which "*affect* security in Europe" was introduced into the mandate of the Stockholm Conference. Military activities carried out outside the European continent — but which affect Europe — cannot be ignored. The zone of application of the CSBMs is an integral element in the process of negotiations. Questions considered as non-negotiable today can become negotiable in the future due to accumulated experience.

3. Deterrence implies the use or threat of force to prevent an enemy from carrying out an aggression. Although it is in many ways an anachronistic concept, global security, as well as European security, is nevertheless based in practice on deterrence. Deterrence itself depends

on perception. Tangible differences of emphasis in the perception of the main components of military security in Europe are of the greatest importance in understanding the position of specific countries in the process of negotiating CSBMs. The WTO states accord priority to steps leading to the physical limitation and reduction of military capabilities and to restraint in military activities. The NATO countries have connected their security mainly with information on military capabilities and structure, with pre-notification on the size and deployment of military forces, as well as with the observation and verification of different kinds of military activities.

Adversaries rarely try to imagine the world and their own actions through their opponent's eyes, although doing so would be to their advantage. Deterrence policy, in order to be effective, has to be credible. To be credible, it should contain a certain indispensible degree of uncertainty. In this context there are some legitimate questions:

- To what extent are confidence and deterrence in the nuclear age compatible?
- Is it possible to reduce CSBMs only to the conventional threat?
- How can one limit negotiable military capabilities to land-based systems and eliminate from the balance the naval and air forces deployed on the adjoining European sea and ocean areas and air space?

These and other questions lead to legitimate skepticism as far as the effectiveness of CSBMs in the purely military field is concerned. Two analysts from the Rand Corporation, in the conclusion of a recent study, suggested: "We should not restrict our definitions of CSBMs to a narrow list of options. We should avoid putting too much emphasis on CSBMs that require a relatively high degree of preplanning, especially at the operational level."[77] The Western approach, as exemplified by the six "amplified" proposals tabled in Stockholm, is rather far removed from this reasonable recommendation.

---

[77]Kevin N. Lewis, Mark A. Lorell, "Confidence-Building Measures and Crisis Resolution. Historical Perspectives," *Orbis,* Summer 1984, p. 306.

4. NATO proposals are considered by the WTO states as intrusive as regards conventional land-based forces, requiring detailed information on the structure of ground forces and land-based air forces, annual forecasts and notifications given 45 days in advance of activities of organized and other organized formations of 6,000 troops (or in case of amphibious activities of 3,000 troops, etc). Nuclear issues are completely excluded, as are independent military activities taking place in adjoining European sea and air space. How can this be reconciled with the fact that American and West European military security is mainly based on nuclear weapons, which are in large measure deployed in the sea and air area adjoining Europe? Adoption of such an approach would establish an imbalance of rights and obligations in favor of one group of countries.

It would be difficult to make a proper evaluation of the problems and obstacles behind the Stockholm negotiations without taking into account the fact that the NATO concept of CSBMs is essentially unbalanced, in that conventional weapons are considered to be the only subject of an eventual agreement. This imbalance is also reflected in the fact that the NATO proposals envisage the possibility of surprise attack from land only, while threats emanating from military activities in the air and on sea are flatly ignored. (How could the Soviet Union ignore the simple fact that the 35 Poseidon and Trident submarines, each with 16 to 24 multiwarhead missiles, by themselves could destroy the Soviet Union many times over?)*

In short, the assumption that surprise attack can come only by land and, furthermore, only by conventional weapons is simply untenable. A successful outcome to the Stockholm Conference requires that these issues be dealt with as directly as possible. Whether this be done through multilateral or bilateral channels, explicitly or tacitly, during the first or second stage of the Conference on CSBMs and Disarmament in Europe, is a secondary consideration. In the final analysis, however, they cannot be ignored.

5. Soviet proposals in Stockholm were directed from the beginning "at removing the risk of nuclear war and lessening the military confrontation."[78]

---

*U.S. President Carter declared before the Congress in 1978 that just *two*: Poseidon nuclear-missile submarines could destroy the 220 cities in the Soviet Union with populations of 100,000 or more.

[78]Statement by Oleg A. Grinevsky, head of the USSR Delegation, Stockholm, January 31, 1984.

The proposals put forward by the Soviet Union embrace obligations on no-first-use and non-use of force, a freeze and reduction of military expenditures, the creation of chemical weapons-free zones and nuclear weapons-free zones in Europe, as well as the development of traditional CBMs (expanding the parameters of the CBMs adopted in Helsinki, including pre-notifications of maneuvers, major military movements and transfers, and some measures of restraint). In contrast to NATO, the CSBMs proposed by the Soviet Union would also be applicable to independent military activities conducted in the adjoining European sea area and air space.

The NATO objections against the inclusion of nuclear (and CW) issues into the negotiations in Stockholm are based on the following reasoning: these are not explicitly envisaged in the mandate of the Conference and are the subject of discussion elsewhere — in the Geneva Disarmament Conference, in the UN and in bilateral Soviet-American talks.

Regarding the first point, it would be difficult and unusual to accept the logic that everything that is not explicitly recommended is prohibited. Western political philosophy usually takes the opposite tack: what is not prohibited is permitted. In the second case, effectiveness and need should be decisive. Formalistic and procedural arguments are usually advanced when the political and conceptual objections are not convincing. This refers especially to the counterarguments associated with the introduction of the non-use of force concept into the Stockholm document. Fortunately, previous NATO rejection and strident criticism of this approach have now been replaced by the more reasonable stance reflected in President Reagan's statement in Dublin (June 4, 1984) and elsewhere emphasizing U.S. and NATO willingness to reaffirm the principle of non-use of force in exchange for certain concessions in the field of military CBMs.[79]

6. N/NA proposals deserve special attention, the former U.S. representative has written, because they have helped to define the "center of gravity" of the Stockholm Conference.[80] The fact that nine of the twelve proposals included in the N/NA document were similar to NATO's does

---

[79]In his address to the UN General Assembly (September 24, 1984), President Reagan said: "...we need to find ways to reduce and eventually to eliminate the threat and use of force in solving international disputes." *The New York Times*, September 25, 1984.

[80]James E. Goodby, "The Stockholm Conference: A Report on the First Year," *Department of State Bulletin*, February 1985, p. 6.

not, however, demonstrate a comparability between the approaches of these two groups of countries in the negotiating process. The three ideas which are not convergent with NATO expectations call for constraints and limitations. These specific proposals, going beyond the NATO approach, are intended to prepare the transition from the "passive" (Helsinki) measures to "active" ones. These CSBMs are aimed at the limitation and reduction of arms and armaments.

7. The prospects for the Stockholm Conference *are* encouraging, if expectations are not exaggerated. The political will necessary to achieve agreement is manifested by the majority of participants, for whom it is important not only to establish a new set of information, notification, and verification measures, but first of all to initiate the process of disarmament.

The Stockholm Conference, which began as a forum for monologues, eventually entered the stage of dialogue and negotiation. At the beginning of 1986, without excessively sharp polemics and confrontations, the sides reached the drafting stage. There have been some signals of readiness, from East and West as well as from the N/NA groups, to complete the work of the first phase before September 19, 1986, not only by businesslike talks on the issues discussed, but also through a meaningful and substantive final agreement. The envisaged outcome of the first stage of the conference (before the CSCE Vienna Follow-up Meeting in November 1986) will probably combine three different expectations:

a) an agreement about the mutual renunciation of the use of force, which will contribute a kind of code of military conduct for the CSCE countries;

b) a commitment on specific confidence- and security-building measures (binding and more substantial than the set of CBMs adopted in the Helsinki Final Act and yet much more limited than those proposed by the NATO countries);

c) some measures of constraint (e.g., diminution of military activity, limitation of number and ceiling of maneuvers, etc.) as postulated by the group of the neutral and non-aligned countries.

Respect for parity and the equal security interests of all CSCE states implies that there will be a direct relationship between the scope of the zone of application and the number and content of CSBMs to be negotiated. The broader the zone, the more ambitious and militarily significant the measures are likely to be.

In sum, the Stockholm Conference should be seen in the broader political perspective of East-West relations. CSBMs will be of rather marginal significance, if not counterproductive, unless integrated with positive changes in the mutual political relations of all major partners involved in the process initiated ten years ago in Helsinki. It is rather ironical, in fact, that the "Conference on *Disarmament* in Europe", though mandated to develop measures of real military significance (such as constraint and disarmament measures), has been confined largely to issues of marginal military significance, such as the modest expansion of the Helsinki CBMs. It is therefore imperative to add to the mandate of the second stage of the CDE the development of genuine disarmament measures in Europe, both in the nuclear and conventional fields. In this light, Gorbachev's Berlin statement of April 18, 1986 was highly instructive. Gorbachev noted, in part, that resistance in Western Europe to removing nuclear weapons from Europe is rooted in the professed belief that, "in this case it would allegedly feel less secure in the face of the conventional armed forces and armaments of the Warsaw Treaty Organization." Gorbachev then observed that "the elimination of nuclear weapons in Europe would create a new situation in Europe not only for the West but also for ourselves...." He then declared:

> The USSR suggests that agreement be reached on substantial reductions in all the components of the land forces and tactical air forces of the European states and the relevant forces of the USA and Canada deployed in Europe. The formations and units to be reduced should be disbanded and their weaponry either destroyed or stored in national territories. Geographically, reductions, obviously, should cover the entire European territory from the Atlantic to the Urals. Operational-tactical nuclear weapons could be reduced simultaneously with conventional weapons.
>
> The question of dependable verification at every stage of this process offers itself. Both national-technical means and international forms of verification, including, if need be, on-site inspection, are possible.[81]

This statement should be viewed as a possible subject of negotiations for Stage II of the CDE, as well as for the Vienna inter-alliance talks on conventional force reductions.

---

[81]*TASS* dispatch, no. 40-1, April 18, 1986.

8. Non-military confidence-building measures are defined as a complex of efforts and actions aimed at strengthening relations of an intersystemic character.[82] The aims of non-military CBMs can be presented as follows:

- efforts to transform an excessively competitive international system into a less hostile one and to establish a more stable political and economic order;

- reduction and elimination of the causes of mistrust, tension and hostility in all fields of international life;

- favoring the creation of more cooperative international environment and the establishment of mechanisms and rules of the cooperation.[83]

In this light a German-Polish document prepared on the occasion of the fifteenth anniversary of the treaty on the normalization of relations between Poland and the Federal Republic of Germany, announced on November 26, 1985, reads:

> In the era of weapons of mass-destruction security cannot be ensured by acting separately against each other, but only jointly, through the policy of partnership in security. It should be based, without any exception, on the application of all principles and provisions of the Helsinki Final Act and the Madrid Concluding Document.
>
> Mutual confidence can be attained only when each of the sides takes into consideration the legitimate interests of the security of the other side.
>
> Efforts in favor of confidence-building should be concrete and encompass all fields on an equal basis: security, economy, science and technology, environmental protection as well as humanitarian areas and others, such as human contacts, information, culture and education.*

In order to achieve these aims, Poland sponsored a UN Resolution on economic confidence-building measures adopted by the General Assembly on December 20, 1983 (No. 38/196). The concept of economic CBMs embraces some elements similar to those of military nature, i.e., an "early

---

[82]See Karl E. Birnbaum, *The Politics of East-West Communication in Europe* (Stockholm, 1979).

[83]See also J.M. Nowak, "Non-Military CBMs in East-West Relations" (in Polish), *Sprawy Miedzynarodowe,* No. 10, 1980, pp. 7-18.

*The document was prepared by a working group appointed by the leadership of the Sejm Deputies Club of the Polish United Workers' Party and the West German Social Democrat faction in the Bundestag.

warning system", a freeze on discriminatory measures undertaken for non-economic reasons in violation of recognized norms of international law, the gradual revocation of such measures, elaboration of provisions for a system of security in international economic relations, etc. These and other measures are of particular significance in the present international debt situation, affecting both debtor and creditor countries.

Another set of non-military confidence-building measures was defined by the UN Declaration on Preparing Societies for Life in Peace (1978). In fact, the entire Helsinki Act and its provisions in all fields of international cooperation might be considered as a charter of confidence-building in East-West relations among all 35 participating states. The process initiated by the CSCE resulted not only in the establishment of regular East-West communication but also in the slow but sure narrowing of differences in many fields, including confidence-building by measures of a military character.

9. Principles for confidence. In the present situation, the confidence-building process can be effective only on condition that some general principles be respected not only in the CSCE area, but in other regions of the world as well. Under the circumstances that have evolved over the past decade, there are chances to restore a genuine detente only if the following requirements are met:

(1) *Respect for the principle of "equal security" and the preservation of military equilibrium.* This demands, above all, acceptance of military parity between East and West and renunciation by all sides of efforts to secure superiority, as the U.S. and USSR reaffirmed during the Geneva summit meeting. It also means refraining from developing one's own security at the expense of the other side, and the treatment of the question of control and verification in a manner adequate to the agreed measures aimed at strengthening security, reducing armaments, and diminishing military activity.

(2) *The effective application of a policy of non-intervention and non-interference in internal affairs.* This involves the renunciation of expansionism and arbitrary recognition of various regions of the world as one's own "security zones" and full respect for the inviolability of existing and recognized frontiers (this concerns, above all, the situation in central Europe).

(3) *The non-use-of-force in international relations.* This concerns both relations between states and between systems. This can be achieved

in different forms: a treaty, or solemn declaration, or any other political act that would ensure the practical effectiveness of the principle of non-use-of-force, particularly a ban on using both nuclear and conventional weapons.

(4) *Separating the ideological competition from interstate relations.* This means refraining from transferring ideological disputes into the sphere of relations between states and from tendencies to impose one's own value system as the only valid model and criterion in evaluating the policies of other states and social movements.

(5) *Joint action aimed at resolving global problems that condition the maintenance of world peace.* This concerns, in particular, steps designed to prevent nuclear war and bring about disarmament. In effect, this means the necessity of joint efforts to limit, reduce and eliminate all kinds of weapons of mass destruction, especially nuclear, and prevent the deployment of weapons in outer space.

There is a growing need for a sober, rational perspective and an honest analysis of the whole complex of contemporary international relations. It is high time that we free ourselves from anachronistic visions of the world in which we are destined to live. We need to see the world as it really is, not as we would wish it to be. We need to stop the prevailing manner of thinking, which causes one to blame the other side for one's own failures and for an unfavorable course of events. Under the circumstances, there is need to become aware both of existing conflicts of interest, which will not disappear, and of common interests and common threats, which demand that a framework for both cooperation and rivalry be developed. Since both global powers have jointly acknowledged that there can be no winners in a nuclear war and have renounced striving for military superiority, the construction of a system of confidence and common security, always an urgent imperative, is now a practical possibility.

APPENDIX OF DOCUMENTS

Excerpts from the
Statement by President Eisenhower
at the Geneva Conference of Heads of Government:
Aerial Inspection and Exchange of Military Blueprints
July 21, 1955*

...The United States Government is prepared to enter into a sound and reliable agreement making possible the reduction of armament. I have directed that an intensive and thorough study of this subject be made within our own government. From these studies, which are continuing, a very important principle is emerging to which I referred in my opening statement on Monday.[1]

No sound and reliable agreement can be made unless it is completely covered by an inspection and reporting system adequate to support every portion of the agreement.

The lessons of history teach us that disarmament agreements without adequate reciprocal inspection increase the dangers of war and do not brighten the prospects of peace.

Thus it is my view that the priority attention of our combined study of disarmament should be upon the subject of inspection and reporting.

Questions suggest themselves.

How effective an inspection system can be designed which would be mutually and reciprocally acceptable within our countries and the other nations of the world? How would such a system operate? What would it accomplish?

Is certainty against surprise aggression attainable by inspection? Could violations be discovered promptly and effectively counteracted?

We have not as yet been able to discover any scientific or other inspection method which would make certain of the elimination of nuclear weapons. So far as we are aware no other nation has made such a discovery. Our study of this problem is continuing. We have not as yet been able to discover any accounting or other inspection method of being certain of the true budgetary facts of total expenditures for armament. Our study of this problem is continuing. We by no means exclude the possibility of finding useful checks in these fields.

As you can see from these statements, it is our impression that many past proposals of disarmament are more sweeping than can be insured by effective inspection.

Gentlemen, since I have been working on this memorandum to present to this Conference, I have been searching my heart and mind for something that I could say here that could convince everyone of the great sincerity of the United States in approaching this problem of disarmament.

I should address myself for a moment principally to the Delegates from the Soviet Union, because our two great countries admittedly possess new and terrible weapons in quantities which do give rise in other parts of the world, or reciprocally, to the fears and dangers of surprise attack.

I propose, therefore, that we take a practical step, that we begin an arrangement, very quickly, as between ourselves — immediately. These steps would include:

To give each other a complete blueprint of our military establishments, from beginning to end, from one end of our countries to the other; lay out the establishments and provide the blueprints to each other.

Next, to provide within our countries facilities for aerial photography to the other country — we

---

*Source: "The Geneva Conference of Heads of Government, July 18-23, 1955"
(Department of State publication 6046, 1955), pp. 56-59.

[1]*Ibid.*, pp. 18-22.

to provide you the facilities within our country, ample facilities for aerial reconnaissance, where you can make all the pictures you choose and take them to your own country to study, you to provide exactly the same facilities for us and we to make these examinations, and by this step to convince the world that we are providing as between ourselves against the possibility of great surprise attack, thus lessening danger and relaxing tension. Likewise we will make more easily attainable a comprehensive and effective system of inspection and disarmament, because what I propose, I assure you, would be but a beginning.

Now from my statements I believe you will anticipate my suggestion. It is that we instruct our representatives in the Subcommittee on Disarmament in discharge of their mandate from the United Nations to give priority effort to the study of inspection and reporting. Such a study could well include a step by step testing of inspection and reporting methods.

The United States is ready to proceed in the study and testing of a reliable system of inspections and reporting, and when that system is proved, then to reduce armaments with all others to the extent that the system will provide assured results.

The successful working out of such a system would do much to develop the mutual confidence which will open wide the avenues of progress for all our peoples.

The quest for peace is the stateman's most exacting duty. Security of the nation entrusted to his care is his greatest responsibility. Practical progress to lasting peace is his fondest hope. Yet in pursuit of his hope he must not betray the trust placed in him as guardian of the people's security. A sound peace — with security, justice, well-being, and freedom for the people of the world — can be achieved, but only by patiently and thoughtfully following a hard and sure and tested road.

Memorandum from the Polish Foreign Minister (Rapacki) to the American Ambassador (Beam) February 14, 1958*

Memorandum

On October 2, 1957, the Government of the Polish People's Republic presented to the General Assembly of the United Nations a proposal concerning the establishment of a denuclearized zone in Central Europe...

The Government of the Polish People's Republic proceeded with the conviction that the establishment of the proposed denuclearized zone could lead to an improvement in the international atmosphere and facilitate broader discussions on disarmament as well as the solution of other controversial internal issues, while the continuation of nuclear armaments and making them universal could only lead to a further solidifying of the division of Europe into opposing blocks and to a further complication of this situation, especially in Central Europe.

In December 1957 the Government of the Polish People's Republic renewed its proposal through diplomatic channels.

Considering the wide repercussions which the Polish initiative has evoked and taking into account the propositions emerging from the discussion which has developed on this proposal, the Government of the Polish People's Republic hereby presents a more detailed elaboration of its proposal, which may facilitate the opening of negotiations and reaching of an agreement on this subject.

I.   The proposed zones should include the territory of: Poland, Czechoslovakia, German Democratic Republic and German Federal Republic. In this territory nuclear weapons would neither be manufactured nor stockpiled, the equipment and installations designed for their servicing would not be located there; the use of nuclear weapons against the territory of this zone would be prohibited.

II. The contents of the obligations arising from the establishment of the denuclearized zone would be based upon the following premises:

   1.   The States included in this zone would undertake the obligation not to manufacture, maintain nor import for their own use and not to permit the location on their territories of nuclear weapons of any type, as well as not to install nor to admit to their territories of installations and equipment designed for serving nuclear weapons, including missiles' launching equipment.

   2.   The four powers (France, United States, Great Britain, and U.S.S.R.) would undertake the following obligations:

      (a)   Not to maintain nuclear weapons in the armaments of their forces stationed on the territories of States included in this zone; neither to maintain nor to install on the territories of these States any installations or equipment designed for serving nuclear weapons, including missiles' launching equipment.

*Source: U.S. Department of State, *Documents on Disarmament, 1945-1959, Vol. II, 1957-1958* (Washington, D.C.: U.S. Government Printing Office, 1960), pp. 944-948.

    (b)   Not to transfer in any manner and under any reason whatsoever, nuclear weapons nor installations and equipment designed for servicing nuclear weapons — to governments or other organs in this area.

3.   The powers which have at their disposal nuclear weapons should undertake the obligation not to use these weapons against the territory of the zone or against any targets situated in this zone.

    Thus the powers would undertake the obligation to respect the status of the zone as an area in which there should be no nuclear weapons and against which nuclear weapons should not be used.

4.   Other States, whose forces are stationed on the territory of any state included in the zone, would also undertake the obligation not to maintain nuclear weapons in the armaments of these forces and not to transfer such weapons to governments or to other organs in this area. Neither will they install equipment or installations designed for the servicing of nuclear weapons, including missiles' launching equipment, on the territories of States in the zone nor will they transfer them to governments or other organs in this area.

    The manner and procedure for the implementation of these obligations could be the subject of detailed mutual stipulations.

III.   In order to ensure the effectiveness and implementation of the obligations contained in Part II, paragraphs 1-2 and 4, the States concerned would undertake to create a system of broad and effective control in the area of the proposed zone and submit themselves to its functioning.

1.   This system could comprise ground as well as aerial control. Adequate control posts, with rights and possibilities of action which would ensure the effectiveness of inspection, could also be established.

    The details and forms of the implementation of control can be agreed upon on the basis of the experience acquired up to the present time in this field, as well as on the basis of proposals submitted by various States in the course of the disarmament negotiations, in the form and to the extent in which they can be adapted to the area of the zone.

    The system of control established for the denuclearized zone could provide useful experience for the realization of a broader disarmament agreement.

2.   For the purpose of supervising the implementation of the proposed obligations an adequate control machinery should be established. There could participate in it, for example, representatives appointed (not excluding additional personal appointments) by organs of the North Atlantic Treaty Organization and of the Warsaw Treaty. Nationals or representatives of States, which do not belong to any military grouping Europe, could also participate in it.

    The procedure of the establishment, operation and reporting of the control organs can be the subject of further mutual stipulations.

IV.   The most simple form of embodying the obligations of States included in the zone would be the conclusion of an appropriate international convention. To avoid, however, implications, which some States might find in such a solution, it can be arranged that:

1.   These obligations be embodied in the form of four unilateral declarations, bearing the character of an international obligation deposited with a mutually agreed upon depository state.

2. The obligations of great powers be embodied in the form of a mutual document or unilateral declaration (as mentioned above in paragraph 1);

3. The obligations of other States, whose armed forces are stationed in the area of the zone, be embodied in the form of unilateral declarations (as mentioned above in paragraph 1).

On the basis of the above proposals the government of the Polish People's Republic suggests to initiate negotiations for the purpose of a further detailed elaboration of the plan for the establishment of the denuclearized zone, of the documents and guarantees related to it as well as of the means of implementation of the undertaken obligations.

The government of the Polish People's Republic has reasons to state that acceptance of the proposal concerning the establishment of a denuclearized zone in Central Europe will facilitate the reaching of an agreement relating to the adequate reduction of conventional armaments and of foreign armed forces stationed on the territory of the States included in the zone.

Excerpts from the
Declaration Submitted by the Soviet Government
at the Geneva Surprise Attack Conference:
Measures for Preventing Surprise Attack
November 28, 1958*

In view of the tense international situation which has become more complex in recent years and in view of the continuing dangerous increase in the rate of rearmament, particularly as regards atomic and hydrogen weapons, the Soviet Government made a proposal regarding the need for a series of urgent measures to be taken by States to limit the arms race, including the cessation of nuclear weapon tests and also the need to reach an agreement on taking measures for preventing the possibility of a surprise attack by one State on another.

In his message of 2 July to President Eisenhower of the United States of America, the Chairman of the Council of Ministers of the USSR, Mr. N.S. Khrushchev, proposed that suitable representatives, appointed by the Governments of the Soviet Union and the United States of America and possibly governments of certain other States, should meet to study the practical aspects of the problem of measures for preventing surprise attack by one State on another and that they should submit their recommendations...

As a result of the agreement which was reached, a conference of representatives of ten States began work on 10 November at Geneva to draft proposals for measures for preventing the danger of a surprise attack. The convening of this conference was received with great satisfaction in all countries, including the Soviet Union, and with the hope that an agreement would be reached at this conference on one of the acute international problems — an agreement whose significance none will deny.

Success in the work of this conference would certainly be an important step towards reducing tension in relations among the States, particularly among the Great Powers, and would contribute to ending the "cold war" and establishing mutual trust. Such success would greatly simplify a solution of other international problems on which it has not yet been possible to come to an agreement...

It is obvious that a reliable system for preventing surprise attacks can only be established after the use of atomic and hydrogen weapons has been prohibited, after such weapons have been eliminated from State arsenals and the stocks destroyed, and also after there has been simultaneously a considerable reduction in conventional weapons and armed forces.

Nevertheless, even under present conditions when the Western Powers, as shown by the experience of many years of talks on disarmament, are not prepared to ban nuclear weapons and considerably reduce their stock of conventional weapons, there is still a possibility to reach agreement on certain practical steps for reducing the danger of a sudden attack. The Soviet Government believes that the basis of these measures could be as follows:

1. The creation of ground control posts.
2. Aerial photography in certain regions.

The reaching of an agreement on these measures is made easier by the fact that the United States of America, as shown in the message of President Eisenhower to Mr. N.S. Khrushchev,

---

*Source: Conference doc. GEN/SA/7/Rev.1, as reproduced in U.N. doc. A/4078 (S/4145), Jan. 5, 1959, Annex 8.

Chairman of the Council of Ministers of the USSR, does not reject in principle the Soviet proposal for creating a system of ground control posts, while the Soviet Union, as stated more than once by the Soviet Government, is in agreement with the proposal for aerial photography in certain regions.

The Soviet Government proposes that an agreement be concluded on the implementation of the following concrete measures:

Ground Control Posts

It is proposed to establish ground control posts at railway junctions, major ports and on main roads, their mission being to see that there are no dangerous concentrations of armed forces and military material at these points...

The Soviet Government believes that the establishment of ground control posts at railway junctions and major ports and on main roads could be one of the effective means of reducing the danger of surprise attack. Hardly anyone would deny that, even with nuclear weapons, preparations for present-day major wars are inextricably linked up with the need to concentrate large military units at certain points, together with great quantities of weapons and military equipment: aeroplanes, tanks, artillery, warships, submarines, land, sea and air transport.

The mission of the ground control posts proposed by the Soviet Union should include making sure that there are no dangerous concentrations of troops and military equipment. This mission is perfectly feasible, since preparations requiring large-scale movements of troops on railways and main roads and through major ports cannot be actually concealed and the establishment of control posts at such points will enable such preparations to be detected in good time.

As for the zone for the establishment of ground control posts, its selection will be determined by the fact that the concentration of troops and military equipment of necessity takes place first and foremost in those areas where heavy contingents of the armed forces of both sides are facing each other, where, as history shows, an outbreak of war is most likely. Europe should be included in such regions since it was the main theater in the last two world wars, and since the main forces of the two military groupings of States — NATO and the Warsaw Treaty organizations — are now concentrated there...

It should also be taken into consideration that, so far as the proposal for ground control posts includes the territories of all parties to the Warsaw Treaty, the zone of these posts should at least include the majority of European NATO countries.

If all States participating in the Geneva Conference agree with the necessity of working out concrete measures for guarding against the danger of a surprise attack, they can also not fail to agree that ground control posts, as one of such measures, should be first and foremost established in Europe...

Aerial photography zones

As one of the measures for preventing a surprise attack, the Soviet Government proposes the establishment of an aerial photography zone in Europe extending 800 kilometers to the east and the west of the line of division between the principal armed forces of NATO and the Warsaw Treaty...

Steps that must be taken by States to ensure effectiveness of measures for preventing a surprise attack

The Soviet Government believes that ground control posts and aerial photography cannot of themselves reduce the danger of surprise attack, particularly with the present types of weapons. This becomes all the more clear if one takes into account the fact that the establishment of ground control posts and the taking of aerial photographs do not affect existing means of surprise attack and would neither lead to a reduction in the number of such means nor to the removal of these devices from certain potentially most dangerous regions.

Ground control posts and aerial photography cannot become effective means of reducing the danger of surprise attack if they are not linked up with steps designed to reduce concentrations of armies of the two opposing politico-military groupings in the potentially most dangerous regions of Europe and to prohibit the siting of the most dangerous types of weapons of mass destruction, at least to begin with, in part of central Europe, that is, in both parts of Germany.

Consequently, the Soviet Government proposes that an agreement be reached on:

a)   a reduction in the size of foreign armed forces on the territories of European States, and

b)   not keeping modern types of weapons of mass destruction on the territories of the Federal Republic of Germany and the German Democratic Republic.

a) A one-third reduction of foreign forces in Europe

To achieve the above aims, the Soviet Government proposes that agreement be reached on reduction by at least one-third of foreign armed forces on the territory of European States lying within the agreed control zone.

No-one will deny that the concentration of foreign armed forces on the territories of European States has been one of the main causes of the present tense situation in Europe which results in the peoples of Europe leading day in day out a feverish existence resembling in many ways life on a volcano...

The reduction of foreign armed forces stationed on the territories of European States by at least one-third would be a first step towards normalizing the situation in Europe...This step would reassure the peoples of Europe and contribute greatly to a decrease in the mistrust poisoning relations among the States.

b) Agreement not to keep nuclear weapons and rockets on the territory of Germany

The policy of keeping nuclear weapons and rockets in European States followed by the leading powers of NATO is an especial danger to European peace. No one will deny this danger which has arisen as a consequence of supplying the armed forces of the NATO States with present-day types of weapons for mass destruction and the conversion of their territories into military strategic springboards. The most serious danger of all for the peoples of Europe resides in the fact that the leading powers of NATO have decided to equip the armed forces of the Federal Republic of Germany in which revanche circles are coming more and more to the fore and concocting plans for armed aggression against their neighbors. This course is at the moment the principal feature of the policy of the Federal Republic of Germany and also of the policies of the Western Powers of Europe although it entails great danger for peace, above all for Western Germany, a fact to which the Soviet Government has repeatedly drawn the attention of the Government of the Federal Republic of Germany.

If we adopt as our pole star the desire to work out practical measures for reducing the danger of surprise attack instead of indulging all the time in empty discussions about this danger, then, in the opinion of the Soviet Government, these measures should be accompanied by an undertaking on the part of States possessing nuclear weapons and rockets not to keep atomic, hydrogen and rocket weapons in either part of Germany where the principal armed forces of the North Atlantic Treaty and the Warsaw Treaty come into contact and where even a minor incident carries within it the danger of grave consequences for the world.

Such an understanding would be in line with the fundamental interests of all European peoples, who are legitimately concerned about the European situation and who realize what catastrophic consequences the use of nuclear weapons could have, particularly in the densely populated regions of Europe. This undertaking would have a good effect on the whole European situation and would contribute to carrying out other measures for removing the threat of war...

The Soviet Government notes with regret that the Western Powers seem to adopt a different approach to the definition of the aims of the Geneva Conference — this is borne out by the draft agenda for the Conference they have submitted. The contents of this agenda amount to a demand that the Conference confine itself to studying existing means of surprise attack: guided missiles, strategic air forces, tactical air forces, ground forces, submarines equipped for discharging guided missiles, etc.

...What is the point of studying devices such as intercontinental rockets if atomic and hydrogen weapons are not banned...The Soviet Government is, as before, ready to agree to a complete ban on atomic, hydrogen and rocket weapons and also to a major reduction in conventional weapons and armed forces and to sign an agreement to that end...

The west does not hide these days...that, in proposing the above agenda for the Geneva Conference, the Western Powers want to find out the war potential of the Warsaw Treaty States, particularly as regards the newest weapons and that they wish to fashion the work of the Conference to this objective. It is a rather blatant desire, as one can see.

But if the Soviet Union and its allies taking part in the Conference were to act in that manner then the final result would be a contest to see who acquires the most military information. It is possible that such information would be of interest to some department of one side or the other, but is that the purpose of the Conference? It is surely clear that the Conference would then achieve nothing but an increase in mutual distrust and suspicion among the Powers.

Naturally the Soviet Government cannot act as an accomplice of those who are striving not for the prevention of the danger of surprise attacks, but for the acquisition of intelligence data on present-day types of atomic, hydrogen, rocket and other weapons at the disposal of the Soviet Union.

The Soviet Government is convinced that, if the participants in the Conference would take into account each other's legitimate security interests and refrain from actions leading to an increase in international tension and mutual suspicion and would make a sincere effort to come to an agreement, an agreement on measures for reducing the danger of surprise attack would be perfectly possible.

For its part, the Soviet Government is ready henceforth to make every effort to see that practical results are achieved at the Geneva Conference as regards measures for reducing the danger of a surprise attack and consequently the danger of a new war.

Excerpts from the
Third Explanatory Document of the Third Point
of the Proposed Plan of Work Submitted by the
Western Experts at the Geneva Surprise Attack Conference:
An Illustrative Outline of a Possible System for
Observation and Inspection of Ground Forces
December 5, 1958*

1. In this paper we consider further those elements of ground forces which are capable of surprise attack as discussed in papers previously tabled by the Western Experts; we identify those technically feasible measures of inspection which could be applied to reduce the danger of surprise attack; and finally we consider the possible effectiveness of such measures.

    1.1. For the purposes of this paper, surprise attack by ground forces is defined as the unexpected assault by ground forces of one state or group of States on another state or group of States in overwhelming strength.

    1.2. In our consideration we were guided by the principle that no participant should alone be responsible for inspection of itself. The assessments contained in this paper are based on this principle.

2. Ground Forces Instruments of Surprise Attack:

    2.1. In papers previously tabled by the Western Experts, some possible instruments of surprise attack used by ground forces were stated to be as follows: Short range surface-to-surface missiles; troop carrier aircraft; armored fighting vehicles; mobile artillery. For convenience, we are considering in this paper all land-based surface-to-surface missiles employing mobile launching devices.

    2.2. In order to apply observation and inspection techniques to the problem of surprise attack by such instruments, it is also necessary to specify the military organizations which use them and the facilities which support them. These include:

    2.2.1   Surface-to-surface missile units employing mobile launchers as distinguished from all other surface-to-surface missiles.

    2.2.2   Armored, mechanized, infantry, airborne, and artillery divisions and brigade groups, including their organic arms and services.

    2.2.3   Headquarters of superior formations.

    2.2.4   Combat and Service Units not in Divisions.

    2.2.5   Supporting logistical facilities including: air bases and airfields (troop carrier); air transport units; supply points, depots and installations: air, rail, road and inland water transport networks and centers.[1]

---

*Source: Conference doc. GEN/SA/10, as reproduced in U.N. doc. A/4078 (S/4145), January 5, 1959, Annex 11.

[1]Certain elements such as tactical aircraft, usually regarded as supporting ground forces are reserved for separate consideration. (Footnote in original.)

2.3 To keep the whole military establishment of any country under constant surveillance is not necessary. It is necessary, however, to establish for the ground forces organization the relative importance of the various elements as possible indicators of attack. It is necessary also to determine which activities in the various elements yield the most useful information of preparation for, or imminence of, surprise attack. The results of one possible analysis of these questions are tabulated at Annex A. The conclusions may be expressed in the following objectives of an inspection system for ground forces:

2.3.1 To establish the location and identity of ground force units, formations, headquarters and installations by verifying reciprocally provided information.

2.3.2 To keep under observation most mobile surface-to-surface missile units, armored and airborne formations, nuclear artillery units, divisions and certain independent units, according to the situation.

2.3.3 To keep under periodic observation the majority of forward and base logistic dumps and installations, and higher headquarters.

2.3.4 To keep under constant observation most air bases (troop carrier), certain major air, rail, road and inland waterway transportation centers, and personnel replacement centers.

2.4 The activities which give information about intention or ability to attack and which, therefore, require to be observed vary in accordance with the nature and function of the element under observation. The main indicators for various elements of ground forces...may be summarized as follows:

Elements		*Indicator*
2.4.1	For all military Elements	Location
2.4.2	For mobile units	Change of location
2.4.3	For armored and airborne and selected samples of infantry and mechanized forces	State of readiness as indicated by strength, equipment, state of training and maneuvers
2.4.4	For combat units, dumps and logistic installations	Logistic activity
2.4.5	For mobile surface-to-surface missiles; nuclear artillery; tank and airborne units	Identification of major armament and transport

2.5 Variations in degree of inspection may be imposed by the following considerations which can only be decided in connection with actual physical situations as known:

2.5.1 Physical position relative to frontier in terms of time into action. Transportation facilities are here relevant.

2.5.2 Balance of forces between forward and rear areas.

2.5.3 Climate including seasonal changes in terms of daylight and darkness, snow, ice, or other conditions affecting operational efficiency and mobility of units observed and of observer teams.

2.6   In conclusion of paragraph 2, it may be remarked that observation near a frontier or of units with high mobility, such as airborne units, results in short warning of attack. Observation of logistic movement and rear units or installations results in a longer warning of general intention but may be ambiguous. In the case of ground forces the value of intensive observation of frontier areas in obtaining last minute warning is diminished by the fact that units stationed near frontiers are usually in a high state of readiness. The longer warning or reassurance given by knowledge of reinforcement capability and logistic activity in rear areas is of comparatively greater value. This leads to the conclusion that general observation including rear areas to a great depth is of greater value in attaining the objective of an inspection system than is intensive observation in a frontier zone alone. There are three advantages to this course:

2.6.1   It gives reassurance of peaceful intent when such is the case (a high state of readiness on frontiers is not unusual).

2.6.2   The warning obtained from deep observation gives earlier advice of an intention to attack and, thus, more opportunity to avert the attack.

2.6.3   The fact of agreement to deep observation is in itself evidence of peaceful intent.

3.   Observation Techniques Applicable to the Problem of Surprise Attack by Ground Forces:

3.1   To reduce the danger of surprise attack by ground forces through the application of observation techniques, these techniques must produce timely data on preparations for and/or launchings of attacks by ground forces. The use of ground observers, resident and mobile, augmented when appropriate by various technical aids to extend their sensory capabilities and complemented by aerial inspection can produce the required data.

3.1.1   The capabilities and reliability of these techniques are influenced by the degree of freedom permitted in applying them as required to all or nearly all of the ground force elements...Observers cannot be relied upon if they are subjected to vetoes or restrictions which limit their activities below a level agreed upon to implement an observation system for ground forces. Their capabilities also are dependent upon having reliable and appropriate communications.

3.1.2   The reciprocal exchange of force data — a "blueprint" — relative to ground forces, such as Order-Of-Battle information and characteristics of logistical systems, is highly desirable and would increase the effectiveness of observers.

3.2   Exchange and Verification of "Blue-Prints" of Force Data:

3.2.1   If a system of exchange of "blue-prints" as discussed in paragraph 3.1.2 above is agreed upon, each participating nation should provide to each other participating nation a statement giving the strength, location and organization of all ground forces units, including their supporting units and logistic installations in such detail as might be considered appropriate. Subsequent changes in the "blue-print" of any significant magnitude should be reported as they are made. A complete and revised "blue-print" should be submitted at specified periods, such as quarterly.

3.2.2   The initial "blue-print" could be verified to the extent deemed necessary by the observing organization, using the methods discussed below.

3.2.3 Aerial inspection techniques...could be used to aid in the verification of "force data" to be exchanged.

3.2.4 In addition to general aerial inspection referred to in paragraph 3.2.3 above, low performance fixed wing and/or rotary wing aircraft equipped, when appropriate, with technical devices such as radar, infra-red or photographic equipment, could provide detailed indications of the presence of military units.

3.2.5 Mobile observers on the ground could be used in order to complete the verification of force data obtained through the use of the techniques mentioned in paragraphs 3.2.3 and 3.2.4.

3.3 Observation of Ground Forces:

3.3.1 Observer teams require freedom of movement into all areas occupied by ground forces at all times, including maneuver areas, using appropriate transportation, including surface vehicles, low performance aircraft and public conveyances, and adequate communication facilities. Operating under these conditions, mobile observer teams could provide the most reliable means of detecting preparations for surprise attack. Observer teams could determine or verify order-of-battle data and establish combat readiness of ground forces including mobile missile units, transportation facilities and logistic installations.

3.3.2 Technical devices, such as mobile radar units and infra-red devices, could be useful in individual cases where a reduction in the number of observers might be made possible.

3.3.3 Aerial inspection techniques, including the use of low-performance aircraft, could increase the effectiveness of the observation program by coverage of ground force movements and of areas in which ground forces are widely dispersed.

3.4 Observation of Transportation Centers:

3.4.1 Resident observers teams at transportation centers could acquire indications of troop and/or logistic build-up. These data could be used to direct mobile observer teams to determine the extent of the build-up.

3.4.2 Resident teams in transportation centers require freedom to move about within the area to which assigned. Resident observers should have the option of using such technical aids as radar or infrared equipment, if desired.

3.4.3 It is considered that observation of transportation centers cannot, of itself, provide adequate reduction in the danger of surprise attack by ground forces, but that it can form a useful part of an overall system for observation of ground forces.

3.5 Communication Facilities:

3.5.1 The information received by observer teams would be transmitted over communication systems having appropriate speed and reliability. The amount of warning received by the defender would depend on the extent of advance preparations, on communication lags, and on the time needed for the pattern of information received at data processing and evaluation centers to be assessed, etc.

3.5.2   In the case of ground force instruments of attack, with few exceptions (such as some missiles), rapidity of transmission of data is not such a critical requirement as with other elements because of the slower reaction time of ground forces and the fact that indicators will usually signify intentions well ahead of time.

3.5.3   In the case of some missiles with mobile launching facilities, the importance of last minute warning must be evaluated in connection with surveillance of other instruments of attack. The level of effort required to acquire and transmit timely data relative to those missiles should be determined in conjunction with analysis of an observation system for missiles with fixed launching facilities.

4.   Summary Evaluation:

4.1   ...The degree of effectiveness of the techniques involved is dependent on the density of observation. The evaluation indicated is predicated on a moderate rather than a very high density. At this density, it is considered that an acceptable degree of dependability is attainable. This implies that all indicators will not be observed at each occurrence, but that the summation of indicators observed in the event of a build-up for surprise attack would provide a high degree of reliability.

5.   Conclusion:

5.1.   Significant reduction of the danger of surprise attack by ground forces is practicable and technically feasible through the use of an adequate number of observer teams with properly defined rights, with proper technical, vehicular and communication equipment, and with unimpeded access to and over areas in which ground forces are located. The number of observers considered adequate for a particular geographic area must be determined in terms of the topography, transportation networks and centers of the area, and the number, types and disposition of the military forces stationed within the area. It does appear that significant results might be obtained even with a modest force of resident and mobile observers. This conclusion is valid so long as the rights of observers as outlined in paragraphs 3.3 and 3.4 are not unduly curtailed. The rights and privileges which observing teams require in order to carry out their task must be agreed in detail.

5.2   We have indicated that we believe that properly applied observation of ground forces can cumulatively provide long term warning of surprise attack by such forces. Insofar as this is true, highly dependable and rapid communication systems are not in this case as important as are the proper organization, disposition and operation of the observation forces.

5.3   However, to take full advantage of the indications of imminent attack given by preparations for missile launching and by the launching itself, an intensity of observation and a speed of communication of a different order from that for ground forces appears to be required. It will be necessary to evaluate the importance of such last minute warning and to determine whether the level of effort required to acquire and to transmit such data for all short range missiles with mobile launchers is worth the cost.

Provisions for Confidence-Building Measures in the Helsinki Final Act.*

93. Document on confidence-building measures and certain aspects of security and disarmament.

94. The participating States;

95. Desirous of eliminating the causes of tension that may exist among them and thus of contributing to the strengthening of peace and security in the world;

96. Determined to strengthen confidence among them and thus to contribute to increasing stability and security in Europe;

97. Determined further to refrain in their mutual relations, as well as in their international relations in general, from the threat or use of force against the territorial integrity or political independence of any State, or in any other manner inconsistent with the purposes of the United Nations and with the Declaration on Principles Guiding Relations between Participating States as adopted in this Final Act.

98. Recognizing the need to contribute to reducing the dangers of armed conflict and of misunderstanding or miscalculation of military activities which could give rise to apprehension, particularly in a situation where the participating States lack clear and timely information about the nature of such activities:

99. Taking into account considerations relevant to efforts aimed at lessening tension and promoting disarmament;

100. Recognizing that the exchange of observers by invitation at military maneuvers will help to promote contacts and mutual understanding;

101. Having studied the question of prior notification of major military movements in the context of confidence-building;

102. Recognizing that there are other ways in which individual States can contribute further to their common objectives;

103. Convinced of the political importance of prior notification of major military maneuvers for the promotion of mutual understanding and the strengthening of confidence, stability and security;

104. Accepting the responsibility of each of them to promote these objectives and to implement this measure, in accordance with the accepted criteria and modalities, as essentials for the realization of these objectives;

105. Recognizing that this measure deriving from political decision rests upon a voluntary basis;

106. Have adoped the following:

I

107. **Prior notification of major military maneuvers**

108. They will notify their major military maneuvers to all other participating States through usual diplomatic channels in accordance with the following provisions:

---

*Source: John J. Maresca, *To Helsinki: The Conference on Security and Cooperation in Europe 1973-1975* (Durham, N.C.: Duke University Press, 1985), pp. 235-239.

109. Notification will be given of major military maneuvers exceeding a total of 25,000 troops, independently or combined with any possible air or naval components (in this context the word "troops" includes amphibious and airborne troops). In the case of independent maneuvers of amphibious or airborne troops, or of combined maneuvers involving them, these troops will be included in this total. Furthermore, in the case of combined maneuvers which do not reach the above total but which involve land forces together with significant numbers of either amphibious or airborne troops, or both, notification can also be given.

110. Notification will be given of major military maneuvers which take place on the territory, in Europe, of any participating State as well as, if applicable, in the adjoining sea area and air space.

111. In the case of a participating State whose territory extends beyond Europe, prior notification need be given only of maneuvers which take place in an area with 250 kilometers from its frontier facing or shared with any other European participating State; the participating State need not, however, give notification in cases in which that area is also contiguous to the participating State's frontier facing or shared with a non-European non-participating State.

112. Notification will be given 21 days or more in advance of the start of the maneuver or in the case of a maneuver arranged at shorter notice at the earliest possible opportunity prior to its starting date.

113. Notification will contain information of the designation, if any, the general purpose of and the States involved in the maneuver, the type or types and numerical strength of the forces engaged, the area and estimated time-frame of its conduct. The participating States will also, if possible, provide additional relevant information, particularly that related to the components of the forces engaged and the period of involvement of these forces.

114. **Prior notification of other military maneuvers**

115. The participating States recognize that they can contribute further to strengthening confidence and increasing security and stability, and to this end may also notify smaller-scale military maneuvers to other participating States, with special regard for those near the area of such maneuvers.

116. To the same end, the participating States also recognize that they may notify other military maneuvers conducted by them.

117. **Exchange of observers**

118. The participating States will invite other participating States, voluntarily and on a bilateral basis, in a spirit of reciprocity and good will towards all participating States, to send observers to attend military maneuvers.

119. The inviting State will determine in each case the number of observers, the procedures and conditions of their participation, and give other information which it may consider useful. It will provide appropriate facilities and hospitality.

120. The invitation will be given as far ahead as is conveniently possible through usual diplomatic channels.

121. **Prior notification of major military movements**

122. In accordance with the Final Recommendations of the Helsinki Consultations the participating States studied the question of prior notification of major military movements as a measure to strengthen confidence.

123. Accordingly, the participating States recognize that they may, at their own discretion and with a view to contributing to confidence-building, notify their major military movements.

124. In the same spirit, further consideration will be given by the States participating in the Conference on Security and Co-operation in Europe to the question of prior notification of major military movements, bearing in mind, in particular, the experience gained by the implementation of the measures which are set forth in this document.

125. **Other confidence-building measures**

126. The participating States recognize that there are other means by which their common objectives can be promoted.

127. In particular, they will, with due regard to reciprocity and with a view to better mutual understanding, promote exchanges by invitation among their military personnel, including visits by military delegations.

128. In order to make a fuller contribution to their common objective of confidence-building, the participating States, when conducting their military activities in the area covered by the provisions for the prior notification of major military maneuvers, will duly take into account and respect this objective.

129. They also recognize that the experience gained by the implementation of the provisions set forth above, together with further efforts, could lead to developing and enlarging measures aimed at strengthening confidence.

II

130. **Questions relating to disarmament**

131. The participating States recognize the interest of all of them in efforts aimed at lessening military confrontation and promoting disarmament which are designed to complement political detente in Europe and to strengthen their security. They are convinced of the necessity to take effective measures in these fields which by their scope and by their nature constitute steps towards the ultimate achievement of general and complete disarmament under strict and effective international control, and which should result in strengthening peace and security throughout the world.

III

132. **General considerations**

133. Having considered the views expressed on various subjects related to the strengthening of security in Europe through joint efforts aimed at promoting detente and disarmament, the participating States, when engaged in such efforts, will, in this context, proceed, in particular, from the following essential considerations:

134. — The complementary nature of the political and military aspects of security;

135. — The interrelation between the security of each participating State and security in Europe as a whole and the relationship which exists, in the broader context of world security, between security in Europe and security in the Mediterranean area;

136. — Respect for the security interests of all States participating in the Conference on Security and Co-operation in Europe inherent in their sovereign equality;

137.   —   The importance that participants in negotiating fora see to it that information about relevant developments, progress and results is provided on an appropriate basis to other States participating in the Conference on Security and Co-operation in Europe and, in return, the justified interest of any of those States in having their views considered.

The "Madrid Mandate" for the
Conference on Confidence- and Security-Building Measures
and Disarmament in Europe*

(From the Concluding Document of the Madrid CSCE Follow-up Conference, September 6, 1983).

The participating States,

Recalling the provisions of the Final Act according to which they recognize the interest of all of them in efforts aimed at lessening military confrontation and promoting disarmament.

Have agreed to convene a Conference on Confidence- and Security-Building Measures and Disarmament in Europe.

1) The aim of the Conference is, as a substantial and integral part of the multilateral process initiated by the Conference on Security and Cooperation in Europe, with the participation of all the States signatories of the Final Act, to undertake in stages, new, effective and concrete actions designed to make progress in strengthening confidence and security and in achieving disarmament, so as to give effect and expression to the duty of States to refrain from the threat or use of force in their mutual relations.

2) Thus the Conference will begin a process of which the first State will be devoted to the negotiation and adoption of a set of mutually complementary confidence- and security-building measures designed to reduce the risk of military confrontation in Europe.

3) The first stage of the Conference will be held in Stockholm commencing on 17 January 1984.

4) On the basis of equality of rights, balance and reciprocity, equal respect for the security interests of all CSCE participating States, and of their respective obligations concerning confidence- and security-building measures and disarmament in Europe, these confidence- and security-building measures will cover the whole of Europe as well as the adjoining sea area[1] and air space. They will be of military significance and politically binding and will be provided with adequate forms of verification which correspond to their content.

As far as the adjoining sea area[1] and air space is concerned, the measures will be applicable to the military activities of all the participating States taking place there whenever these activities affect security in Europe as well as constitute a part of activities taking place within the whole of Europe as referred to above, which they will agree to notify. Necessary specifications will be made, through the negotiations on the confidence- and security-building measures at the Conference.

Nothing in the definition of the zone given above will diminish obligations already undertaken under the Final Act. The confidence- and security-building measures to

---

*Source: Jan Sizoo and Rudolf Th. Jurrjens, *CSCE Decision-Making: the Madrid Experience* (The Hague: Martinus Nijhoff, 1984), pp. 301-302.

[1]In this context, the notion of adjoining sea area is understood to refer also to ocean areas adjoining Europe.

be agreed upon at the Conference will also be applicable in all areas covered by any of the provisions in the Final Act relating to confidence-building measures and certain aspects of security and disarmament.

The provisions established by the negotiators will come into force in the forms and according to the procedure to be agreed upon by the Conference.

5) Taking into account the above-mentioned aim of the Conference, the next follow-up meeting of the participating States of the CSCE, to be held in Vienna, commencing on 4 November 1986, will assess the progress achieved during the first stage of the Conference.

6) Taking into account the relevant provisions of the Final Act, and having reviewed the results achieved by the first stage of the Conference, and also in the light of other relevant negotiations on security and disaramament affecting Europe, a future CSCE follow-up meeting will consider ways and appropriate means for the participating States to continue their efforts for security and disarmament in Europe, including the question of supplementing the present mandate for the next stage of the Conference on Confidence- and Security-Building Measures and Disarmament in Europe.

7) A preparatory meeting, charged with establishing the agenda, time-table and other organizational modalities for the first stage of the Conference, will be held in Helsinki, commencing on 25 October 1983. Its duration shall not exceed three weeks.

8) The rules of procedure, the working methods and the scale of distribution for the expenses valid for the CSCE will, mutatis mutandis, be applied to the Conference and to the preparatory meeting referred to in the preceding paragraph. The services of a technical secretariat will be provided by the host country.

Key Proposals in the Stockholm Conference on Confidence- and Security-Building Measures and Disarmament in Europe (1984/85)

CSCE/SC.1
Stockholm, 24 January 1984

CONFIDENCE- AND SECURITY-BUILDING MEASURES (CSBMs) PROPOSED BY THE DELEGATIONS OF BELGIUM, CANADA, DENMARK, FRANCE, FEDERAL REPUBLIC OF GERMANY, GREECE, ICELAND, ITALY, LUXEMBOURG, NETHERLANDS, NORWAY, PORTUGAL, SPAIN, TURKEY, UNITED KINGDOM, UNITED STATES OF AMERICA

- Recalling that the Conference on Confidence- and Security-Building Measures and Disarmament in Europe is an integral part of the process initiated by the Conference on Security and Co-operation in Europe and that, according to the Madrid Concluding Document, the objective of the first stage of the Conference is to adopt a set of mutually complementary confidence- and security-building measures;

- The above-named States are determined to work for the adoption of measures that would create greater openness and more predictability in military activities in order to reduce the risk of surprise attack, diminish the threat of armed conflict in Europe resulting from misunderstanding and miscalculation, and inhibit the use of force for the purpose of political intimidation;

- Implementation and verification of such measures, as well as respect for existing international commitments, would enhance stability, contribute to the preservation of peace and could open up prospects for new progress in disarmament;

- With these goals in mind and in conformity with the mandate for the Conference the above-mentioned States propose the following confidence- and security-building measures:

I. MEASURES OF INFORMATION

Measure 1: Exchange of Military Information

At the start of each calendar year, the participating States agree to exhange information on the structure of their ground forces and land-based air forces in the zone of application for agreed CSBMs as agreed in the mandate for the Conference.

Information will also be given on the existing regulations in the CDE zone for accredited military personnel.

Clarification of information may be sought by appropriate means.

The information thus exchanged will form a basis for further measures dealing with military activities.

II. MEASURES DESIGNED TO ENHANCE STABILITY

Measure 2: Exchange of Forecasts of Activities Notifiable In Advance

The participating States will exchange annual forecasts of all military activities in the CDE zone which would be notifiable in advance under any other CSBM. Amendments to the forecast need not be given if a notifiable activity is either an addition to or a change from the forecast; such information will be provided in the actual notification for that activity.

Clarification of information contained in the annual forecast may be sought by appropriate means.

Measure 3: Notification of Military Activities

Notification will be given by the participating States 45 days in advance of the following activities in the CDE zone:

- Out-of-garrison land activities.
  When one or more ground force divisions or equivalent formations or 6,000 or more ground troops not organized into a division, or forces comprising more than a specified number of main battle tanks, or armoured personnel carriers/mechanized infantry combat vehicles are carrying out a common activity under a single command, whether independent or combined with air and/or amphibious support.

- Mobilization Activities.
  When 25,000 or more troops or the major combat elements of three or more divisions are involved.

- Amphibious Activities.
  When three or more battalions or 3,000 amphibious troops carry out a landing in the CDE zone.

When a notifiable out-of-garrison land activity, mobilization activity or amphibious activity is carried out on short notice as an alert activity, it will be notifiable at the time it begins, that is, when troops are ordered to carry out the activity.

All notifications will be made in a standardized format to be agreed on.

Compliance with the arrangements agreed under this measure will be subject to various forms of verification including the invitation of observers and inspection. Questions concerning compliance with the arrangements agreed under this measure can be dealt with by appropriate means.

III. OBSERVATION AND VERIFICATION MEASURES

Measure 4: Observation of Certain Military Activities

The participating States agree to invite observers from all other participating States to all pre-notified activities and to alert activities of longer than a specified period conducted in the CDE zone on their territory. The host State shall ensure that observers are provided the opportunity to form a judgement, supported by direct observation in the area of activity, as to the routine nature of the activity.

Measure 5: Compliance and Verification

A. National Technical Means.
  Participating States agree not to interfere with national technical means. In using their national technical means for the purpose of verification, participating States will respect generally recognized principles of international law.

B. Monitoring of Compliance.
  Subject to limitations and modalities to be agreed, participating States may request inspection concerning compliance with agreed CSBMs.

These provisions provide participating States with the opportunity to monitor and thus verify whether notified activities are non-threatening and correspond to the details given in notifications, and that all notifiable activities are properly notified.

Measure 6: Development of Means of Communication

Arrangements should be made which will enhance the means of communication between participating States.

The Delegations of Belgium, Canada, Denmark, France, Federal Republic of Germany, Greece, Iceland, Italy, Luxembourg, Netherlands, Norway, Portugal, Spain, Turkey, United Kingdom, United States of America, as the sponsors of CSCE/SC.1 wish, in the interest of facilitating the work of the Conference, to put forward the following compilation of CSCE/SC.1/Working Documents I-VI amplifying measures 1 - 6 proposed in CSCE/SC.1.

Measure 1: Exchange of Military Information

1. Each participating State will annually exchange information concerning its military command organization, and its regulations for accredited military personnel, in the zone. Such information will be provided to all other participating States and will be exchanged no later than the first day of January of each calendar year, and will be effective as of that date.

2. For each participating State, such information will be provided in writing, and will include the following:

   (a) In chart form, the command organization in the zone, including designation, normal headquarters location in exact geographic terms, and composition of its ground and land-based air forces down to:

      (i) major ground formations and main combat units; and

      (ii) land-based air formations, specifying wing, air regiment of equivalent formations; and

   (b) Its regulations governing the presence and activities in the zone of military personnel accredited to it from other participating States.

3. Clarification of such information may be requested through consultation by appropriate means.

Measure 2: Exchange of Forecasts of Activities Notifiable in Advance

1. Each participating State will exchange annual forecasts of its military activities within the zone for which notification is required by Measure 3 of this document. Such forecasts will be provided to all other participating States. The forecasts, organized into calendar year quarters, will be exchanged for each calendar year, and will be issued not later than the fifteenth day of November for the following calendar year.

2. If a participating State adds a military activity to those that have been forecast or changes information concerning a military activity from that which has been forecast, such additions or changes will be provided in the notification for that activity pursuant to Measure 3.

3. A participating State will present forecasts in writing organized into calendar year quarters, in the following format, for each military activity planned:

   (a) Designation of the activity, including, if applicable, the name of the exercise.

   (b) The general purpose of the activity.

   (c) The thirty-day period during which the activity is planned to begin.

(d)   The names of the participating States that will be engaged in the activity.

(e)   The geographic co-ordinates of the area where the activity is planned to take place.

(f)   The duration of the activity.

(g)   The number of troops, to include amphibious and airborne troops, directing staff, and umpires that will be engaged in the activity.

(h)   The type of forces that will be engaged in the activity.

4. Clarification of information contained in an annual forecast may be requested through consultation by appropriate means.

Measure 3: Notification of Military Activities

A. *General*

1. Each participating State that plans to carry out a military activity, that is, an out-of-garrison land activity, a mobilization activity, or an amphibious activity, in the zone, will give notification 45 days before such activity begins. If a military activity is conducted as an alert, notification will be given in accordance with Section E of this measure. Notifications will be provided to all other participating States.

2. A participating State on whose national territory a military activity is planned to take place will give notification of the entire activity conducted on its territory even if the forces of that State are not engaged in the activity. This will not limit the obligation of other participating States whose participation amounts to a military activity on its own to notify these activities.

3. Compliance with the provisions of this measure will be evaluated on the basis of information exchanged in accordance with Measures 1-3 of this document and will be subject to verification by appropriate means. Participating States will be invited to send observers to military activities within the zone, as provided in Measure 4 of this document. Furthermore, participating States will be permitted to inspect such military activities or possible military activities for the purpose of monitoring compliance, as provided in Measure 5 of this document.

B. *Out-of-Garrison Land Activities*

1. An "out-of-garrison land activity" is an activity in which:

(a)   One or more ground force divisions, equivalent formations, or formations which are temporarily organized into a structure comparable to a division formation, are engaged, if:

(i)   one-half or more of the major combat elements of the division or equivalent formation, that is, tank, infantry, motorized rifle, airborne brigades or regiments or equivalent-sized formations, and at least one supporting artillery or engineer or helicopter element are out-of-garrison at the same time and carrying out a common activity under a single command; or

(ii)   6,000 or more of the troops of the division or equivalent formation are out-of-garrison at the same time and carrying out a common activity under a single command; or

(iii)   (X) main battle tanks or (Y) armoured carriers (AC) of the division or equivalent formation are out-of-garrison at the same time and carrying out a common activity under a single command; or

(b) The combat elements of ground forces not organized into division formations are engaged, if:

    (i) 6,000 or more troops are out-of-garrison at the same time, and carrying out a common activity under a single direct operational command; or

    (ii) (X) main battle tanks or (Y) armoured carriers (AC) are out-of-garrison at the same time and engaged in a common activity under a single direct operational command.

2. Ground forces garrisoned inside of the zone will be considered to be out-of-garrison when they are away from their normal peacetime locations and are in the zone. Ground forces normally garrisoned outside of the zone will be considered to be out-of-garrison when they leave their arrival base within the zone to engage in a military activity on land within the zone.

3. A participating State will give notification of an out-of-garrison land activity whether the activity is independent or combined with air or amphibious support.

4. A participating State will give notification at the start of ground force movements in the case of an out-of-garrison land activity to carry out an activity outside the zone from a point of embarkation inside the zone.

C. *Mobilization Activities*

1. A "mobilization activity" is an activity involving a recall of reservists in which:

(a) 25,000 or more troops, either reservists or reservists in combination with regulars, are involved in the same activity in the zone; or

(b) The majority of the major combat elements, that is, tank, infantry, motorized rifle, airborne brigades or regiments or equivalent-sized formations, of each of three or more divisions or equivalent formations are involved in the same recall activity in the zone.

D. *Amphibious Activities*

1. An "amphibious activity" is any landing from the sea onto the land in which:

(a) A formation equivalent to three or more battalions, whether marine, naval infantry or ground forces, lands in the zone; or

(b) 3,000 or more combat troops land in the zone.

2. If the troops engaged in the landing, as defined in paragraph one, embark in the zone, then the date and place of embarkation will be included in the notification. If the area of landing is changed or decided upon after the initial notification, then that additional information will be given as soon as the area of landing is determined.

E. *Alert Activities*

1. Each participating State carrying out a military activity as an alert will give notification at the time its troops are ordered to carry out the activity.

2. Except as specifically provided, a military activity conducted as an alert will be subject to the same provisions as military activities generally.

F. *Contents of Notifications*

1. A participating State will present notification of a military activity in writing, in the following format:

(a) Description of the activity in the zone, including, if applicable, the name of the exercise.

(b) The name of the headquarters conducting the activity.

(c) The general purpose of the activity, including the relation of the activity to that of any other military activity for which notification is given under this Measure.

(d) The dates and duration of the different phases of the activity in the zone, including the beginning of out-of-garrison deployments, the active exercise phase if applicable, and the recovery phase during which troops are returned to normal peacetime locations, if the recovery phase is to occur immediately after the activity.

(e) The names of the participating States engaged in the activity.

(f) Boundaries of the geographical area in the zone where the activity will take place, including a map trace or geographic co-ordinates.

(g) The number of troops to include amphibious and airborne troops, directing staff and umpires engaged. If more than one participating State engages in the activity, then the number of troops, staff and umpires for each participating State will be specified.

(h) The designation of the ground force divisions engaged in the activity.

(i) The type of other forces engaged in the activity, including ground-based tactical air forces and naval ship-to-shore combat forces, i.e., those executing amphibious operations, air support of ground troops or ship-to-shore gunnery, if part of a military activity in the zone.

(j) Clarifying information if the activity is one for which no forecast was made pursuant to Measure 2 of this document or if the activity is one for which a forecast was made but the informaion provided in the forecast has been changed.

Measure 4: Observation of Certain Military Activities

1. Each participating State will be permitted to send observers to military activities. Observation of a military activity will include observation of all forces participating in the activity, including the forces of participating States other than the host State.

2. *Invitations.* At the time notification of a military activity is given pursuant to Measure 3 of this document, the host State will invite the other participating States to send observers to the activity. A host State need not invite to a military activity observers from a participating State which has given notice to the host State that it does not desire to receive such invitations. A participating State which has given such notice should thereafter receive invitations at any time if it gives notice to the host State of its desire to receive such invitations. A host State need not invite observers to a military activity from a participating State which does not maintain diplomatic relations with the host State.

3. *Duration.* The host State will permit observers to begin observation of a military activity at the time that activity commences. The host State need not permit observation once the end of the activity is reached as indicated in the notification or once the criteria for a military activity pursuant to Measure 3 of this document are no longer met, whichever occurs later.

4. *Alerts.* The participating States need not invite observers to a military activity carried out as an alert unless the alert has a duration of more than 48 hours. If an alert activity has a duration of more than 48 hours, the other participating States will be permitted to observe the alert 36 hours after it begins.

5. *Observer personnel.* A participating State will be permitted to send no more than two observers to a military activity. Each participating State will provide the names of its observers to the host State at the earliest possible time. Wherever possible, at least one of these observers will be from the military personnel of that participating State accredited to the host State.

6. *Protection and immunities.* When in the territory within the zone of any participating State, observers will be granted those diplomatic privileges and immunities necessary to enable them to perform their tasks fully and unhindered at all times. (Details to be decided in the course of negotiations.)

7. *Co-ordination and arrangements.* Invitations to observe a military activity will be issued through diplomatic channels at the time of notification of the activity. Arrangements for observation will be co-ordinated between the host State and the observing State through the embassy of the observing State to the host State, unless those States agree to use another channel.

8. *Co-ordination with other participating States.* Host State responsibilities, other than the responsibility to invite observers, may be delegated by the host State to another participating State engaged in the military activity on the territory of the host State, if that other participating State agrees to assume the responsibility. In such cases, the allocation of responsibilities will be specified in the invitations to observe the activity.

9. *Logistics.* The host State will provide appropriate facilities and hospitality for observers at the site of a military activity being observed.

10. *Transportation.* The host State will provide transportation for observers in the area of the military activity. If requested by an observing State, the host State will provide transportation for observers from the embassy of the observing State or its nearest consulate to the area of the activity. The observing State may use its consular or diplomatic vehicles to transport its own observers to a location designated by the host State, where the observers will transfer to vehicles of the host State. The transfer point will be near a location suitable for observation of the activity.

11. *Communications.* Observers will have access to telecommunication facilities that will allow timely contact with their embassies or nearest consulates.

12. *Scope of observation.*

    (a)   For each military activity, the host State will:

        (i)   guide the observers in the area of the activity;

        (ii)   allow the observers to use personal optical observation equipment necessary to perform their duties;

        (iii)   give detailed briefings on exercise scenarios;

        (iv)   inform the observers of the progress of the activity and provide an opportunity to view directly all formations engaged in the activity;

        (v)   provide other information and observation opportunities sufficient to allow the observers to form a judgement as to the non-threatening nature of the activity.

    (b)   In addition, the host State will:

(i) in the case of out-of-garrison land activities, allow the observers to observe all phases of the activity, including associated air landings, and rail, port and road movements, in the zone between the garrison and the area of out-of-garrison deployment;

(ii) in the case of an amphibious activity, allow observers to observe sea landings and associated air landings from a location on land;

(iii) in the case of a mobilization activity, allow observers to observe the arrival at garrisons of personnel and vehicles; and

(iv) allow the observing State all the rights of observation provided for each type of activity when different types of military activities are combined.

Measure 5: Compliance and Verification

1. Each participating State will use available national technical means of verification in a manner consistent with generally recognized principles of international law.

2. No participating State may interfere with the national technical means of verification of the other participating States operating in accordance with paragraph 1.

3. *Inspections.* Each participating State will be permitted to inspect a military activity or possible military activity within the zone for the purpose of monitoring compliance with agreed CSBMs. A participating State requesting such an inspection will cite the circumstances occasioning its request, and the participating State receiving the request will comply with the request. Any possible dispute as to the validity of this citation will not prevent or delay the conduct of an inspection.

4. *Inspection Quota.* No more than two per participating State per calendar year. An inspection will not be counted if, due to *force majeure,* it cannot be made or is discontinued.

5. *Method of Inspection.* A receiving State will permit inspections from the ground, from the air, or both.

6. *Area for Inspection.* Except as stipulated in paragraph 7, below, an inspecting State is permitted to designate any area for inspection within the territory of a participating State within the zone. Such an area is referred to as a "designated area". In a designated area, the inspecting State will be permitted access, entry and unobstructed survey.

7. *Exceptions.* The receiving State will not be required to permit inspections of any restricted areas. These areas should, however, be as few in number and as limited in extent as possible. In particular, the receiving State will also not be required to permit inspections within:

(a) defence installations, for example, naval bases, dockyards, garrisons, military airfields, firing ranges, buildings or defence research development or production establishments to which access by the general public is normally restricted or denied;

(b) naval vessels, military vehicles or aircraft.

8. *Communication Channels.* The participating States will use diplomatic channels for communications concerning inspections unless the receiving State and inspecting State agree otherwise.

9. *Co-ordination.* In its request, the inspecting State will notify the receiving State of:

(a) the location of the designated area, by giving the geographical co-ordinates of the area;

(b) the mode of transport to and from the designated area;

(c)   whether the inspection will be from the ground, the air, or both;

(d)   information for the issuance of diplomatic visas to inspectors entering the receiving State.

10. *Timing.* An inspection will proceed in the following sequence:

(a)   within 12 hours after the issuance of an inspection request, the receiving State will reply to the inspecting State, make necessary administrative arrangements for the inspection, and transmit co-ordinating information, including the points of entry to its territory. The receiving State will ensure that the inspection team is able to reach the designated area without delay from the points of entry;

(b)   within not less than 24 hours nor more than 36 hours after the issuance of an inspection request, unless otherwise mutually agreed, the inspection team will be permitted to enter the territory of the receiving State;

(c)   the inspecting State will inform the receiving State of any delay in its arrival within 36 hours at the points of entry to the territory of the receiving State and indicate the extra time needed to arrive at the points of entry;

(d)   within 48 hours after the arrival of the inspection team at the designated area, unless otherwise mutually agreed, the inspection will be terminated.

11. *Report of an Inspection.* The inspecting State will prepare a report of its inspection and will provide a copy of that report to all participating States.

12. *Third Parties.* The forces of participating States other than the receiving State within the designated area will be included in an inspection at the discretion of the inspecting State. All participating States will facilitate the passage of inspection teams through their territory.

13. *Inspection Team.* An inspection team will consist of no more than four inspectors, in addition to aircraft crew and one accompanying driver for each land vehicle supplied by the inspecting State. The personnel of the inspection team may be brought into the receiving State by the inspecting State for the purpose of the inspection, or be drawn from the personnel of the diplomatic and consular facilities of the inspecting State in the receiving State.

14. *Transportation.* The inspecting State may provide its own transportation, or, upon request, the receiving State will provide transportation. The inspection team is permitted, unless otherwise mutually agreed, one aircraft and two land vehicles.

15. *Logistic Support.* Upon request, the receiving State will furnish adequate food and lodging for the inspection team. The inspection team may provide their own tents or rations, and may make use of civilian facilities.

16. *Communications.* The inspection team will have access to and may carry telecommunications equipment, the type of which will be subject to the approval of the receiving State.

17. *Equipment.* The inspection team will have the unrestricted use of its own maps, personal optical viewing devices, cameras and tape recorders. The use of other sensors or information-gathering devices for ground inspections is prohibited.

18. *Protection and Immunities.* When in the territory within the zone of any participating State, inspectors will be granted those diplomatic privileges and immunities necessary to enable them to perform their tasks fully and unhindered at all times. (Details to be decided in the course of negotiations.)

19. *Travel with Inspectors.* The receiving State will be permitted to accompany the inspection team

during the period that the team is in the designated area. A representative of the receiving State may travel on each of the vehicles of the inspecting State while the vehicles are moving on land within the territory of the receiving State, and on the aircraft of the inspecting State from the time of the first landing of the aircraft on the territory of the receiving State until the time of the final take-off of the aircraft from the territory of the receiving State.

20. *Modalities for Inspection.* (Other modalities for inspection to be inserted here.)

Measure 6: Development of Means of Communication

1. The participating States will establish dedicated communications links.

2. The participating States may use such dedicated communications links to quickly and directly contact each other for the expeditious handling of the flow of information required by agreed CSBMs.

3. Under certain circumstances, the participating States may use such dedicated communications links for communications on matters of urgency related to agreed CSBMs.

The sixteen sponsors of this document note that this measure should be agreed insofar as the CSBMs finally agreed at the Conference warrant such a measure.

Definitions

1. The "zone" will cover the whole of Europe as well as the adjoining sea area* and air space. As far as the adjoining sea area* and air space is concerned, the measures will be applicable to the military activities of all participating States taking place there whenever these activities affect security in Europe as well as constitute a part of activities taking place within the whole of Europe as referred to above, which they will agree to notify. Necessary specifications will be made through the negotiations on the confidence- and security-building measures at the Conference. Nothing in the definition of the zone given above will diminish obligations already undertaken under the Final Act. The confidence- and security-building measures to be agreed upon at the Conference will also be applicable in all areas covered by any of the provisions in the Final Act relating to confidence-building measures and certain aspects of security and disarmament.

2. A "military activity" is an out-of-garrison land activity, mobilization activity or amphibious activity, in the zone. The definitions of these activities are set forth in Measure 3 of this document.

3. An "alert" is a particular type of "military activity" undertaken without advance notice to the troops involved.

4. A "host State" is a participating State upon whose territory a military activity takes place.

5. An "observer" is a representative designated by an observing State to observe a military activity under Measure 4 of this document.

---

*In this context, the notion of adjoining sea area is understood to refer also to ocean areas adjoining Europe.

6. An "observing State" is a participating State that accepts an invitation under Measure 4 and sends one or more representatives to observe a military activity.

7. A "receiving State" is a participating State upon whose territory an inspection takes place under Measure 5.

8. An "inspecting State" is a participating State that requests an inspection under Measure 5.

9. An "inspector" is a representative designated by an inspecting State to inspect a military activity or possible military activity under Measure 5.

10. Other terms would also have to be defined, including:

    "major ground formations and main combat units"

    "land-based air formations"

    "wing, air regiment or equivalent formations"

    "normal peacetime location"

PROPOSAL SUBMITTED BY THE DELEGATION OF ROMANIA

Confidence- and Security-Building Measures (CSBMs)
(Outline)

In accordance with the aim of the Conference on Confidence- and Security-Building Measures and Disarmament in Europe, as agreed upon by the second CSCE follow-up meeting, which is for this Conference, "as a substantial and integral part of the multilateral process initiated by the Conference on Security and Co-operation in Europe, with the participation of all States signatories of the Final Act, to undertake, in stages, new effective and concrete actions designed to make progress in strengthening confidence and security and in achieving disarmament, so as to give effect and expression to the duty of States to refrain from the threat or use of force in their mutual relations;"

In accordance, also, with the provision of the Concluding Document of the Madrid Meeting, which states that "the Conference will begin a process of which the first stage will be devoted to the negotiation and adoption of a set of mutually complementary confidence- and security-building measures designed to reduce the risk of military confrontation in Europe;"

In view of the prevailing conditions in Europe;

Romania considers that the goal of the first stage of the Conference could be achieved by the negotiation and the adoption of effective measures aimed at:

- elimination of suspicions and the sense of insecurity caused by certain military activities;

- diminution of military activities in the border areas; restraint of military activities generating mistrust and tension; limitation of the geographical area of military activities causing the risk of confrontation;

- extension of information, communication and consultations between States, especially in critical situations.

Such measures should be so formulated as to respond to the criteria provided in the Concluding Document of the Madrid Meeting, which, in turn, are to be so applied as to ensure the attainment of maximum efficiency of these measures. The negotiations could be conceived as a gradual process, aimed at the adoption of an increasingly larger set of measures, in keeping with the relevant provisions of the Concluding Document.

Proceeding from these considerations, Romania proposes the following measures:

I

Notification at least 30 days in advance of military manoeuvres in which take part:
- land or combined forces in excess of (18,000-20,000) troops;
- special forces, such as paratroops and amphibious, in excess of (5,000) troops;
- more than (10-12) surface battle-ships having a total displacement of (50,000-60,000) tons;
- airforce units with more than (45-50) aircraft fighters.

Notification will contain information on the purpose and duration of the manoeuvre, the type of armed forces engaged, numerical strength, armament, combat technique and means of transport, the area of deployment, as well as any other useful information.

Notification at least 30 days in advance of major military movements involving:

- two or more divisions or their equivalent;
- major transportation of heavy armaments and other war material with which two or more divisions or their equivalent could be equipped.

Notification will contain similar information as above.

Prior notification, or as soon as possible in emergency situations, of the placing in a state of alert of national or foreign armed forces or of important components of such forces.

II

Limitation of the armed forces participating in military manoeuvres to a maximum of (40,000-50,000) land troops and establishment of ceilings for the number of battle-ships and aircraft fighters.

Renunciation of multinational military manoeuvres within a zone along each side of the borders between States (width to be determined).

Creation along the borders between States of security zones (width to be determined) in which there would be no manoeuvres, movements or concentrations of armed forces and armaments and no placing in a state of alert of important components of such forces; limitation of the armed forces, armaments and military activities in such regions, as a step towards the establishment of demilitarized zones.

Establishment along the borders between the countries members of NATO and the countries participating in the Warsaw Treaty of a corridor free of nuclear weapons and other weapons of mass destruction (width to be determined) and, in a longer perspective, of any armaments and military activities, except for order and border forces.

Prohibition of manoeuvres and movements of ships and aircraft with nuclear weapons on board within a zone along the land and maritime borders with other States (width to be determined).

Non-stationing of additional troops and non-deployment of additional military bases on the territory of other States, as well as cessation of the extension and modernization of the existing ones.

Encouragement of, and support for the establishment of zones of peaceful co-operation and good neighbourliness, free of nuclear weapons, in the Balkans, in the North of Europe and in other regions of the continent.

III

Establishment of a system of information, communication and consultations among States on problems relating to their security, and prevention and management of crises. Such a system could include:

- consultations between govermental representatives on regular basis and wherever necessary;
- setting-up of a standing consultative body which would meet periodically and in emergency sessions;
- establishment of a system of telephone connections for consultations between the heads of State and government and organization of summit meetings in emergency situations.

Adoption of measures to prevent nuclear conflict by error or accident, including:

- creation of a mechanism of rapid communication between governmental representatives;

- adoption of emergency procedures and development of technical means.

IV

Conclusion of an *all-European Treaty on the non-use or threat of force,* containing concrete provisions and measures designed to give practical effect to the duty of States to refrain from the use or threat of force in their mutual relations. Such a treaty will constitute a corollary of the efforts being deployed at the Stockholm Conference.

Freezing of the military expenditures of States at the level of 1984 until further agreement is reached on their gradual reduction.

Such measures should be accompanied by the prohibition of war propaganda and the encouragement of peaceful relations between States. Systematic information of the public opinion on the progress achieved in the negotiations on confidence- and security-building measures would also contribute to the creation of a favourable climate for the work of the Stockholm Conference.

CONFIDENCE- AND SECURITY-BUILDING MEASURES IN EUROPE

Proposals of the Soviet Union

The situation in Europe and in the entire world requires a radical turn in the policies of States away from confrontation to peaceful co-operation and major practical steps commensurate with the extent of the existing threat to peace.

Attempts to upset the existing military and strategic balance result in a sharp aggravation of international tension and an increased risk of military confrontation, including nuclear confrontation. The continuing deployment of new United States missiles in some West European countries undermines confidence and security in Europe and outside it.

The vital interests of the European peoples and of the whole of mankind require that the relations between nuclear powers be governed by certain norms and that the prevention of nuclear war become the main objective of their foreign policies.

Acting in accordance with the Final Act of the Helsinki Conference on Security and Co-operation in Europe and with the mandate of the present Conference adopted at the Madrid Meeting, the Soviet delegation submits the following proposals and suggestions concerning confidence- and security-building measures in Europe.

I

The participating States of the Conference possessing nuclear weapons should assume an obligation not to be the first to use them. Such an obligation could be assumed unilaterally by each nuclear State which has not yet done so or it could become the subject of an appropriately drafted international agreement.

The assumption of such an obligation and strict compliance with it would equally meet the interests of all States, both nuclear and non-nuclear. It would constitute a measure of paramount importance, leading to a genuine political breakthrough in the field of confidence-building, and that not only among the nuclear powers.

In order to preclude the emergence of situations fraught with the risk of nuclear conflict, provision could be made for the nuclear States participating in the Conference to hold urgent consultations, seek clarifications and provide each other with the necessary information in the event of such a danger arising.

II

The conclusion of a treaty on the non-use of military force and the maintenance of peaceful relations, as proposed by the Warsaw Treaty member States, would be a major confidence-building measure.

The States participating in the Conference could assume such obligations in accordance with their constitutional procedures, irrespective of whether they belong to military alliances, are neutral or non-aligned. Of course, all States of both the Warsaw Treaty and the North Atlantic alliance, military confrontation between whom is particularly dangerous in Europe, should become parties to such a treaty.

An obligation not to be the first to use either nuclear or conventional arms against each other, and hence, not to use military force against each other at all, could form the central provision of the treaty.

Such an obligation would cover the territories of all parties to the treaty, as well as their military and civilian personnel, naval, air and space craft, and other facilities belonging to them, wherever situated. Further, the parties to the treaty should undertake not to endanger the security of international sea, air and space communications passing through areas not covered by any national jurisdiction.

The treaty could also contain other important provisions, aimed at creating confidence, developing co-operation and reducing military confrontation.

The conclusion of the proposed treaty would have a beneficial effect on the development of the entire international situation, would radically reinforce the political and legal foundation underlying compliance with the principle of refraining from the use or threat of force and would enhance the effectiveness of that principle, thereby creating substantive guarantees against the outbreak of military conflicts in Europe, and not in Europe alone.

III

Taking into account the fact that the steep rise in military expenditures intensifies the arms race and imposes an increasingly heavy burden on the peoples, the Warsaw Treaty States on 5 March 1984 addressed a proposal to the NATO member States on the freezing and reduction of military spending in percentage points or absolute figures. Of course, all the States represented at the Stockholm Conference, and especially those possessing major military capabilities, could participate in the efforts to halt the further growth of military spending and reduce it. The resources released as a result of a cut in military spending would be used for the purposes of economic and social development, including assistance to developing countries.

Agreement on that score would constitute a major contribution to confidence building and at the same time provide a realistic means of curbing the arms race.

IV

Ridding Europe of chemical weapons and, above all, not stationing such weapons where there are none at present, as envisaged in the proposals of the Warsaw Treaty member States of 10 January 1984, would help to overcome mistrust between States. The presence of chemical weapons in the densely populated territory of Europe poses a grave threat to all European States and peoples. Given the current aggravation of international tension and the existing risk of the use of chemical weapons, the task of ridding Europe of chemical weapons has become especially pressing.

Such steps would also facilitate agreement to ban chemical weapons and destroy stockpiles of such weapons on a global scale.

V

The Soviet Union takes a positive view of proposals to create nuclear-free zones in various parts of Europe, as is advocated by a number of European States. The creation of a nuclear-free zone in the Balkans, the turning of Northern Europe into a nuclear-free zone, and the establishment of a zone in Europe free from battlefield nuclear weapons on both sides of the contact line between the States of the Warsaw Treaty and of NATO, are directly related to reducing the risk of war and strengthening confidence. These questions deserve serious attention at the Conference.

VI

Taking into account the useful experience gained in implementing the confidence-building measures specified in the relevant provisions of the Helsinki Final Act, it is proposed that a start should now be made on the elaboration of additional confidence-building measures, more significant in nature and broader in scope, specifically such as:

Limitation to a certain numerical level of the scale of ground-force military manoeuvres, conducted independently or jointly with air-force or naval components, including amphibious and airborne troops, in Europe as well as in the adjoining sea (ocean) area and air space.

This measure is all the more pressing since it is difficult to differentiate between modern large-scale military manoeuvres and the preparatory stages of deployment of armed forces for the purpose of commencing hostilities in the European theatre.

Prior notification of major military manoeuvres, exceeding a certain level, of ground, air and naval forces, conducted independently or jointly in Europe and the adjoining sea (ocean) area and air space. In this context the term "troops" also includes amphibious and airborne troops.

Prior notification of major movements and transfers, exceeding a certain level, of ground and air forces in Europe and in the adjoining sea (ocean) area and air space, as well as into this area and out of it. In this context the term "troops" also includes amphibious and airborne troops.

Development of the existing practice of inviting observers from other participating States to attend major military manoeuvres.

In accordance with the mandate, confidence- and security-building measures will be provided with adequate forms of verification which correspond to their content and are to be agreed upon at the Conference.

CSCE/SC.6
Stockholm, 29 January 1985

Working Document
of the Delegation of the Soviet Union

BASIC PROVISIONS FOR A TREATY ON THE MUTUAL NON-USE OF MILITARY FORCE AND THE MAINTENANCE OF PEACEFUL RELATIONS

The objective of an accord on the non-use of military force is to take, in conditions of a persisting nuclear threat, a large-scale step aimed at lessening the danger of military confrontation and facilitating a radical turn in the policies of states away from confrontation to peaceful co-operation.

Reaffirming the obligation they assumed under the United Nations Charter to refrain in their international relations from the threat or use of force, the States participating in the Conference consider it necessary to develop and give concrete form to this principle, and to make it binding to a maximum extent.

Taking into account the fact that the States represented at the Conference on Confidence- and Security-Building Measures and Disarmament in Europe recognized in the Helsinki Final Act the necessity to make the provision on refraining from the threat or use of force an effective norm of international life and undertook to give effect and expression by all the ways and forms which they consider appropriate to the duty to refrain from the threat or use of force in their relations with one another, they now consider it very timely to conclude for that purpose a treaty on the non-use of military force.

1. An obligation not to be the first to use either nuclear or conventional arms against each other, and hence, not to use military force against each other at all, would form the central provision of the proposed treaty.

2. This obligation would mean that the parties to the treaty
- would refrain from any use of military force against another State party, inconsistent with the purposes and principles of the United Nations Charter, in particular from invasion of or attack on its territory;

- would not endanger the security of international sea, air and space communications passing through areas not covered by any national jursidiction.

3. Such an obligation would cover the territories of all parties to the treaty as well as their military and civilian personnel, naval, air and space craft, and other facilities belonging to them, wherever situated.

4. The treaty would bind its parties not to use force against third countries, whether those countries maintain with them bilateral relations of alliance, are non-aligned or neutral.

5. The parties to the treaty would make efforts aimed at preventing a space weapons race, terminating the race in nuclear as well as conventional arms, limiting and reducing arms and achieving disarmament based on the principle of equality of rights, balance and reciprocity, and equal respect for security interests.

6. The treaty could include an obligation for its parties to consider jointly and individually practical measures aimed at preventing the danger of a surprise attack.

7. The parties to the treaty would co-operate in enhancing the effectiveness of the United Nations in fulfilling, in accordance with its Charter, the tasks of peaceful settlement of international disputes and situations of conflict, suppressing acts of aggression, and removing the threat to international peace and security.

8. In the event of the emergence of a risk of war and the use of military force the parties to the treaty would hold urgent consultations, seek clarifications and provide one another with necessary information.

9. The treaty would not limit the inalienable right of its parties to individual and collective defence in accordance with Article 51 of the United Nations Charter.

10. Nothing in the treaty would affect the rights and duties of the participating States under the United Nations Charter, treaties and agreements previously concluded by them.

11. The parties would assume obligations under the treaty in accordance with their constitutional procedures, irrespective of whether they belong to military alliances, are neutral or non-aligned.

12. The treaty would be open for participation in it by all other States that so desired, and would enter into force upon accession to it by all States members of the Warsaw Treaty and of the North Atlantic alliance.

PROPOSAL SUBMITTED BY THE DELEGATIONS OF AUSTRIA, CYPRUS, FINLAND, LICHTENSTEIN, MALTA, SAN MARINO, SWEDEN, SWITZERLAND AND YUGOSLAVIA

on

CONFIDENCE- AND SECURITY-BUILDING MEASURES

The above-mentioned States,

RECALLING that this Conference, which is held within the CSCE process shall take place outside military alliances,

REAFFIRMING their respective policies of neutrality or non-alignment which constitute important contributions to stability in Europe,

EMPHASIZING that their military capabilities by their very structure and organization are solely devoted to national defence purposes and do not present a threat to other States,

STRESSING the need for the respect of the provisions of the Final Act of the Conference on Security and Co-operation in Europe, according to which the participating States will refrain in their mutual relations, as well as in their international relations in general, from the threat or use of force against the territorial integrity or political independence of any State, or in any other manner inconsistent with the purpose and principles of the Charter of the United Nations and the provisions of the Declaration on Principles Guiding Relations between Participating States, in particular from invasion of or attack on its territory,

CONSCIOUS of the need for all participating States to give due attention to the complementary nature of the political and military aspects of security within the CSCE process and to contribute to the efficient and successful work of this Conference,

SUBMIT THE FOLLOWING CONSIDERATIONS:

A) The situation in Europe and the equal respect for the legitimate security interests of every participating State require determined efforts by all of them to build mutual confidence, lessen military confrontation, strengthen security for all and promote disarmament.

B) The measures to be negotiated and adopted in Stockholm should, with the added dimension of security, constitute important progress with respect to the confidence-building measures contained in the Final Act and thereby promote the subsequent negotiations on disarmament.

C) The aim of this Conference is, as a substantial and integral part of the multilateral process initiated by the Conference on Security and Co-operation in Europe, with the participation of all the States signatories of the Final Act, to undertake, in stages, new, effective and concrete actions designed to make progress in strengthening confidence and security and in achieving disarmament, so as to give effect and expression to the duty of States to refrain from the threat or use of force in their mutual relations.

D) The Conference has thus begun a process of which the first stage will be devoted to the negotiation and adoption of a set of mutually complementary confidence- and security-building measures designed to reduce the risk of military confrontation in Europe.

E) The negotiations should be conducive to dialogue and the improvement of communication among the participating States in general, thereby making the Conference in itself a factor of confidence-building and reduction of tensions. Common efforts to increase confidence contribute to achieving security for all participating States.

F) The provision of the Final Act, according to which security in Europe is to be considered in the broader context of world security and is closely linked with security in the Mediterranean area as a whole, should be borne in mind.

G) A balanced set of mutually complementary measures to be negotiated and adopted should - in conformity with the relevant provisions of the mandate - include the further development and enlargement of the confidence-building measures contained in the Final Act and their adaptation to the mandate, as well as qualitatively new confidence- and security-building measures, including *inter alia* constraints on certain military activities.

Concrete measures, such as the following, should be actively considered:

1) Prior notification of major military manoeuvres.

   Substantially improved parameters as compared to those laid down in the Final Act, including earlier prior notification, more detailed information, *inter alia* on the purpose of the manoeuvres, on the units involved and on the level of command as well as parameters relating to the organizational level and/or the number of troops.

2) Prior notification of smaller-scale military manoeuvres which are carried out close to each other in time and space, if the total forces engaged exceed the levels agreed upon under item 1.

3) Prior notification of military manoevres involving amphibious, sea-transported, air-borne, air-mobile forces or combinations thereof.

   The parameters should be significantly lower than for major military manoeuvres and relate to the organizational level, the number of troops and the capacity of their specialized means of tranport.

4) Prior notification of major military movements.

   The parameters should relate to the organizational level, the number of troops and/or the capacity of their specialized means of transport.

5) Prior notification of major military activities, including manoeuvres, in the adjoining sea area and air space, whenever these activities affect security in Europe as well as constitute a part of activities taking place within the whole of Europe and within all other areas covered by any of the provisions of the Final Act relating to confidence-building measures and certain aspects of security and disarmament, which the participating States will agree to notify.

6) Invitation of observers to military manoeuvres and movements subject to prior notification at levels to be determined; improved and standardized conditions for observers.

7) Prior notification of redeployment of major military units as well as of major rotations of military personnel.

The parameters should relate to the organizational level, the number of troops and/or the capacity of their specialized means of transport.

8) Notification of certain other major military activities.

9) Exchange of annual calendars of preplanned major military activities.

10) Ceiling for the forces engaged in a major military manoeuvre or in manoeuvres which are carried out close to each other in time and space.

The parameters should relate to the organizational level and/or the number of troops.

11) Ceiling for amphibious, air-borne, air-mobile forces or combinations thereof engaged in military manoeuvres.

The parameters should be significantly lower than under item 10 and relate to the organizational level, the number of troops and the capacity of their specialized means of transport.

12) Constraints on the deployment in areas to be determined of military units and/or equipment of vital importance for sustained offensive operations.

H) A wide range of confidence- and security-building measures should be subject to negotiation already from the outset. The measure will include adequate verification provisions which correspond to their content.

The negotiations could initially focus on a combination of mutually complementary measures - as illustrated in paragraph G) - on which early agreement might be reached.

I) Such concrete confidence- and security-building measures serve, by their very nature, to give effect and expression to the duty of the participating States to refrain from the threat or use of force in their mutual relations as well as in their international relations in general. They thereby create conditions for considering a reaffirmation, in appropriate ways and forms, of this obligation and the commitment to the peaceful settlement of disputes, undertaken in the United Nations Charter and the Final Act.

J) The Conference could also consider other measures, in conformity with the relevant provisions of the mandate, which are conducive to lessening the risk of military confrontation and the possibility of surprise attack, and to exerting genuine efforts towards containing an increasing arms build-up as well as to strengthening confidence and security and promoting disarmament.

K) Arrangements for dealing with information, notification and rapid exchange of views with regard to measures that may be adopted could be envisaged.

L) The negotiations should take due account of the mandate, according to which the provisions established by the negotiators will come into force in the forms and according to the procedure to be agreed upon by the Conference.

M) A meaningful contribution to the building of confidence would be the undertaking by the participating States to apply the standardized reporting system on military expenditure elaborated by the United Nations.

N) Negotiations should aim at timely and substantial progress in order to provide the Vienna CSCE Follow-up Meeting with sufficient new elements when considering the question of supplementing the present mandate for the next stage of the Conference on Confidence- and Security-Building Measures and Disarmament in Europe in order to deal also with disarmament.

PROPOSAL SUBMITTED BY THE DELEGATIONS OF AUSTRIA, CYPRUS, FINLAND, LIECHTENSTEIN, MALTA, SAN MARINO, SWEDEN, SWITZERLAND AND YUGOSLAVIA

The above-mentioned States,

RENEWING their commitment to document CSCE/SC.3,

EXPRESSING their wish to contribute to the further progress of the Conference,

SUBMIT THE FOLLOWING:

PRIOR NOTIFICATION OF MILITARY ACTIVITIES

The participating States will give prior notification to all other participating States of military manoeuvres, covered by the mandate, i.e.

- the engagement of military formations at or above the notifiable level as defined below outside their normal locations in combat-related exercises and

- movements of such formations at or above the notifiable level between their normal locations and the exercise areas as well as between the areas of the different phases of the exercises.

Such manoeuvres will be subject to prior notification, whenever they involve at least

- numerical total(s) - to be defined - of forces participating in the activity as a whole, emphasizing mobility and firepower or

- one division or equivalent formation* or

- three amphibious, airborne, air-mobile units on battalion level or combinations thereof and a total number of xx troops or a total number of xx troops and a total of yy square metres of shipborne loading capacity.

Prior notification will be given by the participating States on whose territory these manoeuvres take place as well as by those States carrying them out. Prior notification will also be given by States participating in these manoeuvres whenever their participation reaches notifiable level.

Prior notification will be given 42 days or more in advance of the start of these military manoeuvres in a standardized format containing the following information:

1. *General information*

1.1. Type and designation of the activity

---

*For the purpose of the agreement a division or equivalent formation is defined as
- a mobile military unit structured, permanently or temporarily, under one command in headquarters, combat and support elements or
- any other group of forces of equivalent capability
containing 2-5 units on brigade/regiment level with a total number of at least x troops and y tanks/armoured fighting vehicles/helicopters or a total number of at least z tanks/armoured fighting vehicles/helicopters.

1.2. Main purposes

1.3. Timeframe of the activity

1.4. Area of the activity

1.5. Level of command, organizing and commanding the activity

1.6. Participating States

1.7. Number and types of participating divisions or equivalent formations of ground, naval and air forces

1.8. Number and types of participating amphibious, airborne and air-mobile brigades or regiments

1.9. Numerical strength of the activity and the number of troops of each participating State

2 . *Information on participating units*

2.1. Number, types, and, whenever possible, names of units of each participating State involved in the activity, down to and including

- brigade and/or regiment level; equivalent level of ground, naval and air forces

- battalion level in case of amphibious, airborne and air-mobile units

2.2. Numerical strength (manpower) of

- directing staff, including umpires

- each major unit, at

- divisional level or above

- battalion level in case of amphibious, airborne and air-mobile units

2.3. Number and/or type of the following*:

- tanks

- other armoured fighting vehicles

- river crossing and other types of heavy assault engineering equipment

- logistic assault support equipment

- selfpropelled artillery and multiple rocket launchers (more than 100 mm)

- other artillery and multiple rocket launchers (more than 100 mm), as well as mobile surface to air missile launchers

- heavy live ammunition

- combat aircraft

- combat helicopters

- transport aircraft

- transport helicopters

- naval combatants

- landing crafts

- amphibious vessels, including shipborne loading capacity

- auxiliary amphibious ships, including shipborne loading capacity

3. *Information on different phases of the military activity and their geographical definition*

3.1. The starting and finishing dates of the movements of forces involved, whenever they reach notifiable level, as well as the period of absence from their normal locations:

---

*level of detail to be defined

3.2.   Duration of each phase, tactical purpose and corresponding geographical areas, including staging areas, and final positions before returning to their normal locations

4.   *Other information*

4.1.   Additional relevant information to be defined on the units participating in notifiable activities

4.2   Substantial changes and additions to the annual calendar* as well as reasons for such changes

4.3.   Relation to other notifiable activities

4.4.   State responsible for the observation programme.

ANNUAL CALENDAR OF MILITARY ACTIVITIES

The participating States will transmit to all other participating States the calendar of their military activities subject to prior notification and planned for the calendar year beginning on the subsequent January 1st. This annual calendar will be transmitted every year, not later than October 1st, in a standardized format containing the following information:

1. Type of activity

2. Main purposes

3. Timeframe of the activity with envisaged starting and finishing dates

4. Area of the activity

5. Level of command, organizing and commanding the activity

6. States participating in the activity

7. Number and types of the participating divisions or equivalent formations of ground, naval and air forces

8. Number and types of the participating amphibious, airborne and air-mobile units

9. Additional relevant information to be defined on the units participating in notifiable activities

10. Numerical strength of the activity in terms of manpower as well as the number of troops of each participating State.

INVITATION OF OBSERVERS TO MILITARY ACTIVITIES SUBJECT TO PRIOR NOTIFICATION

The participating States will invite observers from all other participating States to military manoeuvres subject to prior notification in accordance with the provisions set out below.

1. The invitation of observers will be extended simultaneously with the prior notification of the military activity.

2. In addition to the basic information on the military activity, given in the prior notification, the invitation will specify

   - State responsible for the observation programme

   - the period of observation

   - the number of observers invited per participating State

   - the languages used in interpretation and translation during the observation.

The deadline for accepting the invitation will be 21 days before the start of the observation. If no reply is given in time, it will be assumed that no observers will be sent.

---

*See below.

3. Additional information will be sent not later than 14 days before the start of the observation to those States which have accepted the invitation or which request such additional information. The information will include

   - basic situation and main phases of the activity
   - maps of the area of activity with a scale to be specified
   - general practical arrangements for the observers
   - authorized equipment for the observers
   - general observation programme.

4. At latest when the observation begins information will be given to the observers on the

   - detailed observation programme
   - directing staff responsible for the observation
   - details of practical arrangements.

5. The observation will cover the duration of the activity, as notified, whenever it reaches the notifiable level, during phases to be defined.

6. The invitation will be valid for at least one observer from each participating State; in case of larger scale activities at least two observers will be invited. In the case of particularly large activities an even higher number of observers could be envisaged.

7. While the observers are on the territory of the State where the activity takes place, their persons and property, as well as their living quarters, will be granted the same privileges and immunities as those accorded to diplomatic agents in the Vienna Convention on Diplomatic Relations.

8. The invited State decides whether to send military and/or civilian observers.

9. Observers from all participating States will be treated without discrimination and offered equal opportunities to carry out their functions.

10. Observers will be given the possibility to use high capability optical equipment to be defined.

11. The use of photographic equipment is generally prohibited, unless the inviting State grants exceptions.

12. Irrespective of the language(s) used in briefings and information, it/they will be interpreted or, respectively, translated into at least one working language of the CSCE. Languages to be used will be indicated in the invitations given.

13. The observers will be given extensive and authoritative information on the purpose, the basic situation and the progress of the activity through detailed daily briefings with the help of maps and drawings describing the current situation.

14. In particular the observers, in order to evaluate whether the activities are carried out in conformity with the prior notification and whether they are non-threatening in nature, will be given opportunity

   - to observe ground, naval and air units carrying out the main activities as well as areas that are essential for the above purposes of observation
   - to visit, within the framework of alternatives offered, field units on levels to be defined and to follow their activities and to communicate with commanders and troops
   - to be briefed on unit levels, to be defined, by commanders or members of their staff
   - to be provided with information concerning their approximate position, geographically and in relation to units referred to in earlier briefings.

They will be provided with appropriate means of transportation.

15. The inviting State will also consider requests made by other participating States before the start of the observation programme with regard to possibilities to supplement the observation programme in order to meet particular concerns expressed.

16. The inviting State will guide the observers in the area of activities. Observers will follow the relevant instruction issued by the inviting State in accordance with the provisions set out in this document. The inviting State will not be required to permit observation of restricted installations such as fortifications or similar defence sites.

17. Observers will be given the opportunity to communicate with their embassies and/or with their home authorities.

18. The inviting State will cover the costs of board and lodging during the observation programme.

NOTIFICATION AND OBSERVATION OF MILITARY ACTIVITIES CARRIED OUT AT SHORT NOTICE

1. The participating States will give notification to all other participating States of military manoeuvres as defined on page [174], covered by the mandate, which are carried out at short notice, whenever they reach notifiable level as defined on page [174].

2. The participating States will give notification to all other participating States of such military movements which are not in conjunction with combat-related exercises, of military formations at or above notifiable level to and from normal locations/staging areas, covered by the mandate, whenever they reach notifiable level as defined on page [174].

3. Notification will be given by the participating States on whose territory these manoeuvres and movements take place as well as by those States carrying them out. Notification will also be given by States participating in these manoeuvres and movements whenever their participation reaches notifiable level.

4. Notification will be given at the earliest possible opportunity prior to the start of these manoeuvres and movements in a standardized format containing information as outlined under the section on prior notification with exceptions to be defined.

5. The participating States will invite observers from all other participating States to military manoeuvres carried out at short notice, when the duration of the activity at or above notifiable level exceeds ... hours, in accordance with provisions to be elaborated.

CONSTRAINTS ON CERTAIN MILITARY ACTIVITIES

1. The participating States will abide by the following constraints on the notifiable military activities referred to in this section:

2. No individual military manoeuvre will exceed five times the notifiable level and its duration at or above notifiable level will not exceed 17 days.

3. The States will neither permit on their own territory nor carry out or participate in more than a total of five notifiable military manoeuvres per calendar year which are of a size less than two times the notifiable level; moreover, the States will neither permit on their own territory nor carry out or participate* in a total of more than one such manoeuvre at the same time.

    However, if such manoeuvres are notified in the annual calendar by the States on whose territory they take place as well as by those States carrying them out, the total number per calendar year and the number of such manoeuvres taking place at the same time will not be restricted.

---

*to be defined

4.　The States will neither permit on their own territory nor carry out or participate* in more than a total of five military manoeuvres per calendar year, which are of a size of two times the notifiable level or above. Such manoeuvres will be notified already in the annual calendar by the States on whose territory they take place as well as by those States carrying them out.

The States will neither permit on their own territory nor carry out or participate* in a total of more than two such manoeuvres at the same time. However, once a year two such manoeuvres may be combined but not exceed a total of seven times the notifiable level.

OBSERVATION UPON REQUEST OF MILITARY ACTIVITIES

A participating State which considers that its national security interests are at stake or that the continued effectiveness of the agreement is seriously jeopardized because of specific circumstances in the context of the implementation of measures contained in the preceding sections, will be entitled to request to send observers to another participating State on very short notice.

The request will be addressed to the State on whose territory the activities or presumed activities are carried out. It will define the requested observation area and cite the relevant measures on which the request is based as well as state the reasons for the request.

The State which has received such a request will, within twelve hours after receiving the request, invite the requesting State to carry out the observation. The modalities and guidelines for such observation, including exceptions which apply to restricted areas, will be defined.

If, for reasons of supreme national security interests, a State which has been requested to receive observers would find itself compelled not to grant the request, it will state the reasons which in the particular situation have caused the refusal in an answer addressed to the requesting State within twelve hours after receiving the request.

In view of the fact that the CSCE process takes place outside military alliances, the requested State will in addition invite observers from a third participating State with which it does not maintain relations of military alliance.

If observers from a third State take part, they will participate in the whole observation together with the observers from the requesting State, and be provided with the same facilities.

After a requested observation has been carried out, the requesting State, the inviting State as well as the invited third State, will each submit a report to the other participating States within ... hours upon completion of the observation.

The request and the answer thereto as well as the reports on the observation will be transmitted in acccordance with the provisions contained in the following section.

ARRANGEMENTS FOR DEALING WITH INFORMATION, NOTIFICATION AND RAPID EXCHANGE OF VIEWS WITH REGARD TO THE MEASURES TO BE ADOPTED

1.　General provisions for communication

Each participating State will transmit all communications foreseen in the preceding sections to all other participating States.

Such communications can be transmitted in conformity with the modalities for rapid communications set out below.

The participating States can also make use of the rapid communication system in order to provide and request clarification and additional information as well as in order to exchange views concerning the implementation of the measures in the preceding sections.

---

*to be defined

2. *Modalities for rapid communications*

In order to ensure that the communications can be transmitted without delay and at all times, the participating States will keep telecommunication lines accessible between the designated representatives of the participating States for transmitting and receiving printed text, charts and maps.

Access to all such communications will be restricted in accordance with CSCE practice.

CONSULTATIVE ARRANGEMENTS

Arrangements for short meetings of representatives of all the participating States, in relation to the implementation of the measures in the preceding sections, should also be envisaged.

Such meetings could be convened

- on an ad hoc basis, at the request of any participating State, to deal with exceptional situations
- at intervals and dates to be decided by the participating States, to proceed to an exchange of views on the routine implementation of the measures.

NON-USE OF FORCE

The participating States stress their commitment to the Final Act of the CSCE and the need for improved and consistent implementation of all its provisions, and thus to further the process of increasing security and developing co-operation in Europe, thereby contributing to international peace and security in the world as a whole. They are also conscious of the interrelation between security in Europe as a whole, and security in the Mediterranean area.

All the principles set forth in the Final Act are of primary significance and, accordingly, will all be equally and unreservedly applied, each of them being interpreted taking into account the others. Respect for these principles will encourage the development of normal and friendly relations and the progress of co-operation among the participating States in all fields.

The participating States are conscious of the complementary nature of the political and military aspects of security within the CSCE.

They stress that the principle of refraining from the threat or use of force is a universally recognized obligation in international law, binding all States, and that non-compliance with it consequently constitutes a violation of international law.

They reaffirm their determination to respect this principle, contained in the Final Act, so as to ensure that, as a norm of international life, it is strictly and effectively observed. No consideration may be invoked to serve to warrant resort to the threat or use of force in contravention of this principle.

They recall the inherent right of individual or collective self-defence if an armed attack occurs.

The participating States will refrain, in their mutual as well as in their international relations in general,

- from the threat or use of force against the territorial integrity or political independence of any State, or in any other manner inconsistent with the purposes of the United Nations and with the Final Act, and, accordingly,

- from any manifestation of force, direct or indirect, for the purpose of inducing any State to renounce the full exercise of its sovereign rights,

regardless of this State's political, social, economic, or cultural system and irrespective of whether or not they maintain with this State relations of alliance.

No territorial occupation or acquisition resulting from the threat or use of force will be recognized as legal.

The participating States stress their firm commitment to the principle of peaceful settlement of disputes as contained in the Final Act, convinced that it is an essential complement to the duty of States to refrain from the threat or use of force. They reaffirm their resolve to settle exclusively by peaceful means any dispute existing or arising between them. They also express their determination to reinforce, improve and develop the methods at their disposal for the peaceful settlement of disputes.

The participating States confirm the universal significance of human rights and fundamental freedoms, the respect for which is an essential factor for the CSCE process and for international peace and security as well as for the development of friendly relations and co-operation among themselves as among all States.

The participating States confirm that they will refrain from direct or indirect assistance to terrorist activities or to subversive or other activities directed towards the violent overthrow of the regime of another participating State. They express their determination to take effective measures for the prevention and suppression of acts of terrorism and will take all appropriate measures in preventing their respective territories from being used for the preparation, organization or commission of terrorist activities, including measures to prohibit on their territories illegal activities of persons, groups and organizations that instigate, organize or engage in the perpetration of acts of terrorism.

The participating States will fulfil in good faith their obligations under international law. They declare that their existing international commitments, rights and obligations do not conflict with the present document.

They confirm that in the event of a conflict between the obligations of the members of the United Nations under the Charter of the United Nations and their obligations under any treaty or other international agreement, their obligations under the Charter will prevail.

The participating States are convinced that the situation in Europe and the equal respect for the legitimate security interests of every participating State require determined efforts by all of them to build mutual confidence, lessen military confrontation, strengthen security for all and promote disarmament.

By their very nature concrete CSBMs serve to give effect and expression to the duty of States to refrain from the threat or use of force.